PRAISE FOR
Local is Our Future

"There is no more important task than re-localizing our economies – it will help to cure everything from climate change to human sadness. And this book will tell you how it's done, with testimony from some of the world's most remarkable pioneers."
– **Bill McKibben**, author of *Falter: Has the Human Game Begun to Play Itself Out?*

"Helena Norberg-Hodge, one of the great visionary voices of our time, explains in clear and simple detail why you, your children, and the vast majority of the world's people find it nearly impossible to make a decent living, while Earth dies and a few already obscenely wealthy individuals grow their fortunes by billions each year. Drawing on inspiring examples from around the world, she goes on to spell out what we the people, standing together, can do about it. A must read book for our time."
– **David Korten**, author of *When Corporations Rule the World* and *Change the Story, Change the Future: A Living Economy for a Living Earth*

"If we are ever going to solve today's enormous and escalating problems, we will need to radically rethink the economy. The argument for economic decentralization, powerfully and passionately presented in this fine book, is one that we can no longer ignore."
– **David Suzuki,** biologist, broadcaster and environmental activist

"Globalization is often seen as an aspiration or an inevitability. This book suggests otherwise. With clear, concise reasoning and vivid examples, it offers localization as a potent conceptual lens and action principle to reverse the ruin of culture, nature, and place around the world."
– **Charles Eisenstein**, author of *Sacred Economics* and *The More Beautiful World Our Hearts Know is Possible*

"At a time when any thinking person would have good reason to despair, Helena Norberg-Hodge provides a wonderfully positive vision of the future. The key message of this book is simple, but revolutionary: by bringing the economy closer to home, we are both helping to heal the Earth and breathing new life into our increasingly divided com-

munities. This beautiful new narrative is one of empowerment and active hope."
– **Joanna Macy**, co-author, *Active Hope: How to Face the Mess We're in without Going Crazy*

"A terrific overview of the problems embedded in a globalized economy, and the ways real people in real places can begin the journey back to prosperity."
– **Douglas Rushkoff,** Professor of Media Theory and Digital Economics

"Don't be fooled by the slimness of this volume: the wisdom contained in these pages, which reflect a lifetime of Helena Norberg-Hodge's work in dozens of countries, has the power to pull Earth back from the brink. She shows how restoring community economies is the essential building block for global prosperity, resilience, and justice. Read it, share it with your friends, and join the global movement for economic localization!"
– **Michael H. Shuman**, author of *The Local Economy Solution* and *Local Dollars, Local Sense*

"Helena Norberg-Hodge is a systems thinker with international experience, whose call for 'big picture activism' cuts right through the conventional divide of left-right politics, to breathe life into our outdated notions of progress and development. This book offers hope and inspiration, as well as pragmatic and strategic guidelines for structural change in both the global North and South."
– **Camila Moreno**, climate researcher, author of *Carbon Metrics and the New Colonial Equations*

"By waging war on both cultural and biological diversity the global economy threatens the very marrow of life itself. By contrast, as this wonderful little book makes clear, localisation is Nature's greatest friend and supporter. *Local is Our Future* provides caring and clear-minded guidance to help us restore and heal the Earth."
– **Stephan Harding,** author of *Animate Earth*

"Helena Norberg-Hodge and her team around the world are the champions of a decentralised, sustainable, healthy and local economy. Helena's books and films have inspired hundreds of thousands of people in all corners of the globe. In this small and beautiful book Helena

presents the case for a local and imaginative economy in compelling and convincing manner. Without any doubt the future is local, and once you have read this book you will know in no uncertain terms why. So read this book and give it as a present to your friends, colleagues and companions. Solutions to many of our environmental, social and personal problems are to be found under our feet."
– **Satish Kumar,** Editor Emeritus, *Resurgence & Ecologist* and founder of Schumacher College

"Local is indeed our future, and Helena Norberg-Hodge shows us how to get there. As she makes clear, it's all about connection: with each other, with Nature, with place. This is an essential guidebook, lighting the way towards economies of human and ecological well-being. And as we confront climate change, our very survival."
– **Judy Wicks,** author of *Good Morning, Beautiful Business* and cofounder of the Business Alliance for Local Living Economies (BALLE)

"*Local is Our Future* is an inspirational manifesto. Globalization is destroying our communities and our planet, but Helena presents a compelling, positive solution that I completely endorse."
– **Alice Waters,** restaurateur and local food activist

"Helena has been at the forefront of warning us about the dangers of economic globalization and the unbridled power of corporations, while at the same showing how radical alternatives in the form of localized economies are very real utopias, not pipe-dreams. This book lays out a clear critique of the madness of 'development', and describes pathways towards a more just, sustainable future. Essential reading for all, especially millennials and other youth growing up in today's confusing times."
– **Ashish Kothari,** a founding member of the environmental group Kalpavriksh and co-author of *Churning the Earth: The Making of Global India*

"Localisation – a very important antidote to globalisation – is the only hope for the future. If our civilization collapses, which is a very real threat, humanity will be able to survive only by adopting the principles of localisation, and if we want to avoid its collapse, we must adopt them urgently. Read this book!"
– **Iain McGilchrist,** psychiatrist and author of *The Master and His Emissary*

HELENA
NORBERG-HODGE

LOCAL IS OUR FUTURE

Steps to an
Economics of Happiness

LOCAL FUTURES

Local Futures works to renew ecological, social and spiritual well-being by helping to show the way towards a genuinely sustainable future – one of interconnected, localized economies. Our flagship **Economics of Happiness** program provides a range of educational and practical tools for communities and concerned citizens, and links a broad array of initiatives, alternative institutes and networks worldwide.

Published by Local Futures
USA, UK, Australia, Mexico
www.localfutures.org

Design: Robert MacDonald, Information Outfitter
Front cover concept: Laura Tyley
Cover photo: Catarina Belova / Shutterstock
Author photo: John Page

Library of Congress Control Number:
CIP data available from the publisher upon request.
ISBN 978-1-7329804-0-2

Printed in the United States of America on acid-free paper.
10 9 8 7 6 5 4 3

CONTENTS

ACKNOWLEDGEMENTS

I have been promoting economic localization for more than four decades now, so the framing and core ideas of this book are mine. However, the process of getting those ideas on paper has been a collaborative effort. I am privileged to have working with me at Local Futures a truly remarkable team of bright, caring and capable people. For this book I am particularly grateful to four of them. My long-term friend and colleague Steve Gorelick played a central role. His patience and superb editing skills, combined with help in structuring and laying out the basic arguments, were of vital importance. I was also supported by Henry Coleman's drafting and creative writing skills. Carly Gayle provided invaluable help in research and editing, while my ever-present assistant of fifteen years, Marjana Kos, not only supervised the whole project but provided much-appreciated feedback. Finally, my partner in all things, John Page, constantly encouraged me to produce something not just valuable, but readable. I hope we succeeded.

1

RECLAIMING THE FUTURE

For our species to have a future, it must be local.

The good news is that the path to such a future is already being forged. Away from the screens of the mainstream media, the crude 'bigger is better' narrative that has dominated economic thinking for centuries is being challenged by a much gentler, more 'feminine', inclusive perspective that places human and ecological well-being front and center. People are coming to recognize that *connection*, both to others and to Nature herself, is the wellspring of human happiness. And every day new, inspiring initiatives are springing up that offer the potential for genuine prosperity.

At the same time there is a growing awareness – from the grassroots to academia – that the real economy is the natural world, on which we ultimately depend for all of our needs. Only when we embrace a structural shift in the current economy – away from dependence on a corporate-run global marketplace, towards diversified local systems – will we be able to live in a way that reflects this understanding.

Tragically, our political and business leaders remain blind to these and other realities. They are taking us down a different path, one where biotechnology will feed the world, the internet will enable global cooperation, and robots will free people from the drudgery of physical and mental effort. They believe that life was brutish and hard before the modern era of global trade and mega-technology, and that only through ever more economic growth can our most pressing problems be solved.

A companion belief is that another technology – money – can somehow generate wealth out of thin air. This fantasy is embedded deep within the global economic system, a system built upon trillions of dollars of debt backed by nothing but more debt. We also have leaders who are convinced that enriching the 1% will somehow 'trickle down' to benefit the poor. They point to arbitrary measures – GDP, per capita income, the availability of consumer goods – whose rise 'proves' that their policies are working. But the reality is that the rich have gotten richer than ever, while the majority must work harder and faster just to provide their families with shelter, education and medical care.

The path of progress through technology that was supposed to save us time has, ironically, succeeded in *robbing* us of our time: we all must work at the speed of the available technology. This is leaving people ever more stressed, and taking a tremendous toll on our connection to others, to the natural world and even to ourselves.

But instead of questioning the role of the economic system in severing these connections, people tend to blame themselves for not managing their lives well enough, for not spending enough time with family and friends. In addition to feeling guilty, we often end up feeling isolated because the ever more fleeting and shallow nature of our social encounters with others fuels a show-off culture in which love and affirmation are sought through such superficial means as plastic surgery, designer clothes and Facebook likes. These are poor substitutes for genuine connection, and only heighten feelings of depression, loneliness and anxiety.

The dominant narrative of 'progress' fails to capture these psychological costs. Just as importantly, it also omits the looming threats of climate chaos, species extinction and the collapse of ecosystems worldwide. The truth is that, in fundamentally important ways, conditions have actually worsened, year by year, for several decades now.

Why has this happened? In the last 40 years the world has undergone a process that has been more momentous than the industrial revolution – and yet most of us have been only dimly aware of it. That process is known as *economic globalization*. Built largely through 'free trade' treaties that free up or deregulate global banks and businesses, it has exponentially increased the exploitation of both human and natural resources, with impacts that no techno-fix can hope to alleviate.

Consider what has happened in the political sphere. Even nominally democratic countries have been subjected to what amounts to a series of coup d'états that systematically siphoned power away from elected governments into the hands of deregulated global business and finance. International bodies like the World Trade Organization, the World Bank, the International Monetary Fund and even the COP climate negotiations have become centers of power for a de-facto global government of multinational corporations and banks – one that is wholly unaccountable to citizens or communities. Every step of the way, this path has taken us further and further from the natural world and from real democracy; it is leading to the disintegration of the social fabric, and to epidemics of divisiveness, fear, addiction and violence.

In most quarters, the enormous significance of systematic deregulation remains poorly understood. At neither the governmental nor the grassroots level has this process been examined from a global perspective. Even climate activists have largely overlooked the fact that globalization has led to a massive increase in CO_2 emissions from global trade – emissions that do not appear in any nation's carbon accounting.

Our collective ignorance has led many to blame human nature or overpopulation, rather than the economy, for all the destruction we see in our world. I hear people ask, "What is wrong with humans – why are we so greedy and selfish?!" They often conclude, "The human race has become a cancer. Maybe we don't deserve to survive."

As the global economic system has grown bigger and bigger, it has become extremely difficult for us to see what is actually happening. Many of our basic needs have criss-crossed the planet several times before we purchase them: how can we know whether they were produced under fair and humane labor conditions, or what impact their production had on the environment? Even within academia, knowledge has become so specialized that 'experts' know little beyond the narrow focus of their single discipline. Corporate funding, meanwhile, helps push students into business administration or STEM subjects – science, technology, engineering and math – while interdisciplinary approaches, ecology, the humanities and experiential knowledge are pushed to the margins.

With giant corporations and media conglomerates gaining so much wealth and power, they have been able to shape not only government and academic policy, but also public opinion and intellectual discourse. Targeted corporate funding has even influenced the environmental movement: as we'll explore in greater depth in Chapter 11, corporations have set the agenda for the global environmental movement, encouraging NGOs and nation-states to shift their focus away from fundamental political change, towards market solutions like green consumerism, ethical investment, and carbon trading – pseudo-solutions that ensure corporate power remains unchallenged.

In the era of fully-fledged globalization, what is 'economic' has become absurd. Fish from Europe are flown to Asia to be deboned, then flown back to Europe to be sold. Hundreds of thousands of tons of hay grown on irrigated land in drought-stricken southern California are shipped to China.[1] England and Australia recently exchanged 20 tons of bottled water, just with each other.[2] These examples of insane trade are no longer outliers: they are now typical of how the global economy operates.

And yet very few people are aware of this. Instead, narrow reductionism, linked to ever larger-scale structures, has enabled a global techno-optimist narrative to dominate discussions of humanity's future. From Netflix to TED talks, from Washington, DC to Silicon Valley, the cliché of a high-tech, totally global – even interplanetary – society continues to be trumpeted as the singular destiny of our species.

What does this future look like? Google's Ray Kurzweil informs us that our food will come from "AI-controlled vertical buildings" and include "in-vitro cloned meat". According to Tesla's Elon Musk, building a city on Mars is "the critical thing for maximizing the life of humanity", while "30 layers of tunnels" will relieve congestion in Earth's high-density cities. Goldman Sachs explains that the digitization of everyday objects will "establish networks between machines, humans, and the internet, leading to the creation of new ecosystems that enable higher productivity, better energy efficiency, and higher profitability".

These ideas are lauded as visionary and bold, but what they promise is simply the escalation of dominant trends – neo-colonial expansion, urbanization and commodification – turbocharged with fancy gadgets. What they don't tell us is that, at every level, the system is dumping the most abundant natural resource of all – human energy and labor – on the waste heap. At the same time, our taxes are subsidizing a dramatic increase in the use of energy and scarce natural resources. We have a system that is simultaneously creating mass unemployment, poverty and pollution.

This system is not the expression of the will of the majority: on the contrary, we have been actively excluded from having a say. But I do not believe that a 'good guys vs. bad guys' narrative is accurate either. It is true that the people consciously pushing corporate monoculture represent only a tiny fraction of the global population – perhaps less than 10,000 individuals worldwide – but even they are so mesmerized by abstract economic models and indicators that they are often blind to the real-world effects of their decisions.

In a sense, the system has entrapped us all. Even the CEOs of large corporations and banks are driven by speculative markets to meet short-term profit and growth targets – they are under intense pressure to stay on top for fear of losing their own jobs and letting down their shareholders. So it is the system itself that must be called to account and changed – not the interchangeable individuals who wield power within it.

But as I said at the outset, this is not the only direction in which the world is being taken. People around the globe are yearning for the deep bonds of community and connection to nature that we evolved with for most of our existence. And from the bottom up they are pushing for a fundamental shift in direction. Theirs is not a vision built upon a few billionaires' fetish for high-tech gimmicks and knack for money-accumulation: instead it emerges from a deep experience of what it means to be human.

At the grassroots on every continent, people in their diverse cultures are coming together to reweave the social fabric and to reconnect with the Earth and her ecosystems. They are building prosperous local economies and intergenerational communities that provide more meaningful, productive work. From community gardens to farmers markets, from alternative learning spaces to local business alliances and co-ops – what all these have in common is a renewal of place-based relationships that reflect an enduring and innately human desire for love and connection.

These localization initiatives emphatically demonstrate that human nature is not the problem – on the contrary, it is the *in*human scale of a techno-economic monoculture that has infiltrated and manipulated our desires and our needs. This understanding is reinforced by observing what happens when people come back into contact with human-scale structures; I have seen prisoners transformed, delinquent teenagers given meaning and purpose, depression healed, and social, ethnic and intergenerational rifts bridged.

In many cases, these initiatives stem more from common sense than any intention to 'change the world'. But together they nevertheless present a powerful challenge to the corporate order, and articulate a very different vision of the future.

My organization and I are in the fortunate and all-too-rare position of receiving news of new localization projects every week, from all corners of the globe. But just as most people are ill-informed about globalization, most are also largely ignorant of the rapid proliferation of localization projects. Even those directly involved in these efforts can feel isolated and that they are swimming against the current. But stepping back and looking at the bigger picture can leave one amazed at what people power is accomplishing. Given the huge systemic supports for the big and the global, from lavish government subsidies and tax breaks to corporate-owned media and heavy biases in funding for academia, the continued flourishing of these alternatives is a testimony to the power of community – to the motivation, perseverance and strength that emerges when people come together to create positive change. What's more, many individuals and groups are uniting to form larger networks – particularly around the 'new economy' – that focus on loosening the corporate stranglehold on our institutions so that we may begin to shift systemic supports to favor decentralized economic systems. Such shifts would help cultivate more empowered, more diverse and more vital communities and democracies worldwide.

This emerging movement transcends the conventional left-right dichotomy. It is about enabling diverse human values and dreams to flourish, while simultaneously re-embedding culture in nature. It means societies can move towards withdrawing their dependence on distant, unaccountable monopolies that produce our basic needs in high-input, mechanized monocultural systems on the other side of the world, in favor of local and artisanal production for local needs. The emphasis here is on *real* needs, not the artificial wants created by marketers and advertisers in an effort to stoke the furnaces of consumerism and endless growth.

Localization means getting out of the highly unstable and exploitative bubbles of speculation and debt, and back to the real economy – our interface with other people and the natural world. Rather than demanding countless tons of perfectly straight carrots and discarding the ones that do not fit the bill (as supermarket chains do), local markets require a diversity of products, and therefore create incentives for more diversified and ecological production. This means more food with far less machinery and chemicals, more hands on the land and therefore more meaningful employment. It means dramatically reduced CO_2 emissions, no need for plastic packaging, more space for wild biodiversity, more circulation of wealth within local communities, more face-to-face conversations between producers and consumers and more flourishing cultures founded on genuine interdependence.

This is what I call the 'solution-multiplier' effect of localization, and the pattern extends beyond our food systems. In the blind, disconnected and over-specialized system of global monoculture, I have seen housing developments built with imported steel, plastic and concrete while the oak trees on-site are razed and turned into woodchips. In contrast, the shortening of distances structurally means more eyes per acre and more innovative use of available resources. It may sound utopian, but as we withdraw dependence on highly centralized, automated systems in fields like healthcare and education, we can rebalance the ratios between doctor and patient, between teacher and student, and thereby make space for individual needs and capabilities.

It is entirely reasonable to envisage a world without unemployment; as is true of every price-tag on a supermarket shelf, unemployment is a political decision that, at the moment, is being made according to the mantra of 'efficiency' in centralized profit-making. As both political left and right have bought into the dogma of 'bigger is better', citizens have been left with no real alternative.

When we strengthen the human-scale economy, decision-making itself is transformed. Not only do we create systems that are small enough for us to influence, but we also embed ourselves within a web of relationships that informs our actions and perspectives at a deep level. The increased visibility of our impacts on community and local ecosystems leads to experiential awareness, enabling us to become both more empowered to make change and more humbled by the complexity of life around us.

At a fundamental level, localization allows us to appreciate the constantly evolving, changing nature of the universe. Instead of living by labels – seeing the world through words, fixed concepts and numbers – we become aware that every person, animal and plant is unique and changing from moment to moment. Localization lends us the intimacy and pace required to feel this fullness, and to feel the joy of being an integral part of a living web of relationships.

My direct experience of a localized way of life, and my subsequent motivation to raise the alarm about globalization, came about quite by chance. In 1975, I went to Ladakh, or 'Little Tibet', as part of a film team, just as the region was thrown open to the global economy. As a linguist, I quickly became fluent in the Ladakhi language, enabling me to experience this ancient culture almost from the inside. When I arrived, Ladakh's community- and nature-based economy still provided people with a sense of self-esteem and control over their own lives; I soon came to realize that the Ladakhis were among the freest, most peaceful and joyous people I had ever met. What's more, their happiness translated into a remarkable tolerance – an acceptance of difference and of adversity.

Over the next decade I was a first-hand witness to the devastating impact of economic development. I came to see how the modern economic system centralizes power and creates intense competition for artificially scarce educational opportunities and jobs, while at the same time reaching deep into the psyches of young children, perverting a universal need for love and acceptance into a need to consume. In Ladakh, this proved a deadly combination, leading within a decade to depression and suicide, violent conflict, and the ravaging of nature.

Motivated to get the word out, I gave public talks around the world, and, with newfound clarity, saw the many ways in which globalization was affecting the industrialized world too. Returning to my native country of Sweden, I was shocked that an American company – Phillip Morris – held extensive control over the Swedish food system, and that most people had no idea this was the case. Nor could most Swedes imagine that massive subsidies for large-scale production and long-distance transport – already underway in the 1970s – had made it economically 'efficient' to truck potatoes to Italy to be washed before packaging them in plastic and sending them back to be sold.

17

After several years of meeting with various organizations and community leaders around the world, I became aware that the lack of genuine dialogue between global North and global South – so-called 'rich' and 'poor' countries – sustained a false narrative about 'progress'.

In the global South, people fall prey to propaganda that shows the North American and European lifestyle to be leisurely, glamorous and trouble-free – a false narrative that is immensely destructive to cultural and individual self-esteem. At the same time, many people in the global North fall for the illusion that corporations and governments have cleaned up their act on environmental fronts. In the late 1980s and early 90s, for example, environmental groups celebrated the improving water quality of rivers like the Thames in London and the Hudson in New York, not realizing that the newfound freedom of capital to comb the world for the most investor-friendly environments meant that most of the North's dirty industry had moved to where labor was cheapest and environmental standards were lowest. We weren't really cleaning up the environment; we were merely outsourcing the pollution. Far from reducing ecological harm, there was a seismic *increase* in pollution and emissions, not least because the distances goods now had to travel from producer to consumer increased immensely.

A similar deception was going on with jobs. While the abandoned workforces in the North were told that their jobs had gone to benefit the poor on the other side of the world, it was mainly the elite in the South that benefited from corporate expansion, while the majority saw their land-based economies undermined. Millions were pushed into urban slums where they competed with one another for jobs producing goods for Northern consumers – often in slavery-like conditions.

I have found that people with a foot in both parts of the world can see more clearly the destructive impact of globalization. But we all have an obligation to inform ourselves about the realities on the ground, and to critically question the narratives about global growth and technological progress that wash over us daily.

There are two diametrically opposing paths before us. One is leading us relentlessly towards fast-paced, large-scale, monocultural, techno-development. It's a path that separates us from each other and the natural world, and accelerates our downward social and ecological decline. The other path is about slowing down, scaling back and fostering deep connection, in order to restore the social and economic structures essential for meeting our material and deeper human needs in ways that nurture the only planet we have.

2

GLOBALIZATION
Creating a
Lose-Lose World

economic globalization. *noun. 1. the deregulation of trade and finance in order to enable businesses and banks to operate globally; 2. the emergence of a single world market dominated by transnational companies (often confused with international collaboration, interdependence, global community.)*

In order to understand why localization is such a strategic way forward, we need to better understand the process of globalization, to which localizing is a fundamental alternative.

For some, 'globalization' connotes a borderless world, where new technologies facilitate the free flow of ideas and innovation. To others, it means an interconnected planet in which webs of trade relationships make every nation interdependent with every other nation, for the good of all. For still others it means a 'global village' – a peaceful, cooperative planet shrunk to human scale.

If these high-minded images sound overly rosy about globalization, it's because they originated in corporate-friendly think tanks. If they seem familiar, it's because they've been disseminated widely by corporate-controlled media.

A more objective view is that globalization, at its core, is an economic process. It's about deregulating trade and investment – primarily through trade treaties that free up big businesses and banks to enter and extract wealth from local markets worldwide. As we'll see in the following chapters, handing more power to global corporations and banks is not fostering better commu-

21

nication and leading to an interdependent global village: it is leading instead to conflict, violence and right-wing hyper-nationalism, to an erosion of diversity and an unraveling of the natural world.

When the first modern 'free trade' treaties were proposed, globalization was described as inevitable: opposing it, the public was told, made no more sense than opposing continental drift. Awareness has grown over the years of the many problems globalization has spawned, but we are now told that "there's no going back" – that the same process that created these problems is the only way to solve them.

Since this book advocates for an alternative to the supposedly unstoppable process of globalization, I want to remind the reader that the globalized system is, in fact, man-made, and therefore can be changed. The course that has been set for us is neither inevitable nor fixed, and we can choose to shift direction.

The fact is, the road to corporate monoculture has been carefully designed: rules and regulations have been altered to make it possible, and subsidies and tax incentives enacted to drive it forward. Even today, rules are being rewritten in order to enable global banks and businesses to enter still more local markets, to enclose still more of the public commons, to strip more power from democratic institutions, and to exploit still more of the natural world.

500 years of globalization

It's often thought that globalization began relatively recently. Some point to the creation of the World Bank, the IMF, and the GATT (precursor to the World Trade Organization) in the aftermath of World War II. Others look to the first 'free trade' treaties, ratified in the 1990s. But globalization is essentially a continuation of the conquest and colonial exploitation that began 500 years ago – a process that relied upon genocide, slavery, and the destruction of local economies and cultures.

Today, corporate deregulation gives multinational businesses and banks the freedom to move in and out of national economies in search of cheap labor and resources, low taxes, and lax environmental and social protection measures. Although this is less overtly brutal than conquest and colonialism, the goal – the extraction of wealth to benefit a small elite – is the same, as are the impacts on local economies and cultures.

Why have governments acquiesced to this process? One important reason is that as corporate power has grown, local businesses and the jobs they provided have been decimated. National, state and even municipal governments need jobs for their citizens, and see little option but to try to lure the jobs that corporations promise. They do so by rolling out the red carpet for multinationals in the form of tax breaks, subsidies and skewed regulations. Since other governments are competing for the same corporate jobs, they are often willing to scale back labor, health, and environmental regulations in an effort to make themselves more attractive to big businesses. The economist Jeffrey Sachs, an authority on economic development and poverty, explains how this process works:

"When capital becomes internationally mobile, countries begin to compete for it. They do this by offering improved profitability compared with other countries, for example, by cutting corporate tax rates, easing regulations, tolerating pollution, or ignoring labor standards. In the ensuing competition among governments, capital benefits from a 'race to the bottom,' in which governments engage in a downward spiral of taxation and regulation in order to try to keep one step ahead of other countries. All countries lose in the end, since all end up losing tax revenue and regulations needed to manage the economy. The biggest loser ends up being internationally immobile labor..."[1]

The subsidies and tax incentives that governments offer global businesses can be huge. When Amazon, one of the world's richest corporations, dangled the prospect of an estimated 50,000 jobs in front of cities all over North America, more than 230 state and municipal governments submitted bids. These included New Jersey ($7 billion in tax breaks), Montgomery County,

Maryland ($6.5 billion in tax breaks plus $2 billion in infrastructure improvements), and Atlanta ($2 billion in incentives, including an Amazon-only executive lounge at the city's airport). The winning bids, from New York City and Arlington, Virginia, promised the corporation nearly $5 billion in tax breaks (though New York has since removed itself as a candidate).

A *New York Times* investigative report found that state and local governments in the US provide over $80 billion per year in tax incentives, free public land, infrastructure assistance, low-cost financing and other subsidies to attract and retain large, non-local businesses. These subsidy programs are administered "almost exclusively to the benefit of big corporations (aided by highly paid lobbyists) at the expense of small businesses."[2]

Bidding wars for the favors of a particular corporation represent just one small part of the way global businesses are subsidized – as we'll see in Chapter 9, there are many indirect subsidies as well, including fossil fuel subsidies that make global transport artificially cheap. The net result is that the components assembled into everyday products come from factories or subcontractors in numerous countries thousands of miles apart. It has been estimated, for example, that the components of a single iPhone have traveled a combined 500,000 miles before reaching the end user.[3]

Overall, deregulation has led to an explosion in international trade, which was over twenty-eight times greater in 2017 than in 1950.[4] This has massively enriched multinational businesses and banks, while criminally wasting resources, pumping out pollution and CO_2 emissions, and imposing high-input, monocultural production the world over.

Much of this trade, especially in food, is redundant. In a typical year, the US exports millions of tons of beef, potatoes, and other foods, while importing nearly identical amounts of each.[5] This pattern of importing and exporting similar products has been documented in many other countries as well. In some cases, it is literally the same product that is both exported and imported: the New York Times reports that "Cod caught off Norway is shipped to China to be turned into filets, then shipped back to Norway for sale." That's a 10,000-mile round-trip journey.[6]

Financial deregulation

In tandem and completely interlinked with the growth in global trade, the deregulation of finance is allowing ever larger flows of capital to enter and leave nations at the click of a button. Between 1980 and 2007, cross-border flows of capital rose from $500 billion to a peak of $11.8 *trillion*.[7]

This hyper-mobile capital has turned currency and commodities markets into a global casino in which billions can be made by investors, at great cost to national and local economies.

Most people remain unaware that almost all the money in circulation today is backed by nothing but debt.[8] Speculative bets using borrowed money can yield profits that can be invested in still larger bets. Despite increased awareness of this madness after the 2008 global financial meltdown, all major economies today have higher levels of borrowing relative to GDP than they did in 2007.[9]

All told, the enrichment of multinational businesses has reached unprecedented extremes. Although they are unaccountable to any electorate, many of these corporations are now so big that they wield more economic and political power than national governments: of the 100 largest economies in the world in 2016, 69 were corporations.[10] In 2018, the revenue of a single company, Shell, was larger than the GDP of 138 individual countries.[11] Nonetheless, the United States government alone provides between $10 billion and $52 billion per year in subsidies and tax cuts to large oil companies – Shell included.[12] Between cashed-up lobbyists, free trade treaties and the 'revolving door' between government and the highest echelons of industry, corporate rule has become the norm, even in so-called democracies.

Are corporations really becoming more powerful than elected governments? Consider the Investor State Dispute Settlement

(ISDS) clauses that are now standard in 'free trade' treaties. These rules allow corporations to challenge any national policies – including domestic labor laws that mandate humane working conditions or rules that limit pollution of air and water – if they might reduce the corporation's expected profits. Tobacco giant Philip Morris filed such a suit against the Australian government, which had required changes to cigarette packaging in the name of public health. (See "Trade deregulation", Chapter 9.) Because of international trade treaties signed and ratified over the last several decades, most nations are now bound up in agreements that force them to acquiesce to the demands of big corporations and banks, or to engage in costly legal battles that take place in secretive, corporate-friendly arbitration tribunals outside of their own domestic courts.

Like Frankenstein's monster, globalization is an out-of-control man-made creation – the product of systemic blindness and narrow, specialized knowledge. It has enabled the biggest businesses and banks in the world to blindly pursue their own priority of narrow, extractive profit-maximization – and to grow ever more powerful as a result.

If allowed to proceed, globalization will continue to have wide-ranging negative impacts that point towards the collapse of human communities and Earth's living systems. The next chapter will outline these consequences, drawing fundamental links between the global economy and the many forms of breakdown we are experiencing today.

3

COUNTING
THE COSTS

The structural forces described in the previous chapter have led to an increasingly globalized economy that, in the long term, has no winners. Among the first losers have been small farmers, the poor, and the disenfranchised. But as the economic, social and environmental costs of globalization mount, not even the wealthy few can escape its impact: they too must survive on an ecologically degraded planet and suffer the consequences of a social fabric ripped apart.

Here are just some of the costs of globalization:

■ Loss of livelihoods
When corporations can roam the world looking for cheap labor, no one's job is safe. The impact of NAFTA is a case in point. The Economic Policy Institute estimates that by 2013, NAFTA had resulted in a net loss of 682,900 jobs in the US.[1] At the same time, Mexican family farmers were also hit hard by the trade agreement: as heavily-subsidized US corn flooded into Mexico, the price received by Mexican farmers for their production fell by over 60 percent from the 1990s to 2005.[2] Nearly 5 million jobs on family farms were lost, with a net loss of 2 million jobs in the entire agricultural sector since NAFTA's inception. The supposed benefits of the trade agreement are hard to discern: despite the new factory jobs on the US-Mexican border (where people toil under sweatshop conditions, disconnected from community), the unemployment rate in Mexico was higher in 2014 than 1994.[3]

Even within national borders, jobs are lost when a global corporation displaces local businesses. That's because big businesses use far less labor than their smaller competitors for the same amount of output. For example, studies have shown that every new supermarket in the UK entails a net loss of 276 jobs.[4]

Online marketing – a major feature of the global economy – also costs jobs. The internet retailer Amazon currently employs about 23 people for every $10 million in retail sales, while independent retailers employ 57 people for the same amount of sales.[5] According to a study by the Institute for Local Self-Reliance, Amazon has so far destroyed 150,000 more jobs than it has created.[6]

Advances in technology also cost jobs. The most obvious example is in manufacturing, where robots have replaced a wide range of skilled workers. But technology is having a similar impact on agriculture: for decades, farmworkers have been displaced by ever more sophisticated technology, but the latest advances – GPS-guided and computer-connected tractors – are making farmers themselves obsolete. Already in the US, the Census Bureau considers farmers such a demographically insignificant population that it no longer tracks their numbers.[7]

Any discussion about what's happening to livelihoods is incomplete unless we also ask what a 'job' is in the modern world. For example, the most important activity for human survival and well-being – parenting – has been systematically marginalized over many generations now, turning it into a type of shadow work that is rated at 'zero' in the national accounts. Much the same has happened to food production: unless cash changes hands, the food produced – whether in one's backyard or in reciprocal exchange with other members of the community – also rates a 'zero'.

In the global South, where reciprocal exchange is still common, this faulty accounting is particularly devastating because it justifies government policies that pull people out of rural villages – where they can produce their own food and have networks of community support – into sprawling urban slums. They may now be living in real poverty, but if they earn even a dollar a day at a 'job', no matter how demeaning, it is seen as an improvement because what they had before was 'zero'. In the commercialized global economy, in other words, jobs and livelihoods without a price tag on them are not valued at all, nor are the people who do those jobs.[8]

■ Declining health

Globalization is contributing to a decline in our physical well-being. Societies in the West are experiencing unprecedented rates of obesity, diabetes, heart disease and cancer, with the elite in developing countries fast catching up. Processed food – genetically modified, laden with pesticide residues, preservatives, artificial flavorings and processed fats, and nutritionally depleted from long-term storage and long-distance transport – contributes significantly to these problems. So do pollution, sedentary jobs and being cut off from a sense of support and community.

The corporate-controlled technologies that have arisen in tandem with globalization also carry health costs. Many industrial agricultural inputs are proven to be carcinogenic, while others contain endocrine disruptors that are extremely toxic even in minute amounts. Microwave radiation from the use of cell phones and wireless devices has increased exponentially in recent years, with potential health impacts that have yet to be adequately studied.

The global economy also relies on massive and ever-increasing amounts of energy, with a wide range of associated health impacts. The effects of fossil fuel dependence include elevated rates of pollution-related respiratory diseases and 'cancer alleys' near refineries. The health impacts of nuclear power will be felt near Japan's Fukushima plant for generations to come, and the millions of tons of spent fuel and low-level radioactive material piling up at other nuclear plants will remain hazardous for thousands of years.

■ Psychological costs

Every day, communities in the less-developed parts of the world are bombarded with media images that present the modern,

Western consumer lifestyle as the ideal, while implicitly denigrating local traditions and land-based ways of life. Global advertising expenditures exceeded $500 billion in 2016, with the highest rate of spending growth occurring in the less-industrialized countries of the South.[9] These images send the message that the urban is sophisticated and the rural is backward; that imports of processed food and manufactured goods are superior to local products; that "imported is good, local is crap," in the words of an advertising executive in China.[10]

People are not only being lured to abandon local foods for McDonald's hamburgers and local dress for designer jeans; they are being induced to remake their own identities to emulate the glamorous blonde-haired, blue-eyed stars of Hollywood films and American-style advertising. For the vast majority around the world, living up to this artificial ideal will prove impossible. Attempts to do so can result in a profound sense of failure, inferiority and self-rejection.

Individuals in the West – the supposed epicenter of glamour – are subjected to the same pressures. No matter who you are or where you live, the global consumer monoculture imposes an ideal that is impossible to attain, fueling feelings of insecurity that make it easier for corporate marketers to sell products promising to make you more attractive, popular, and 'cool'.

Children bear the brunt of this process, with drug abuse, violence and suicide steadily rising in the under-18 age group in many industrialized countries. Psychological damage also manifests itself in body image issues, self-harm or addiction, or outwardly expressed as anger and aggression. These behaviors can be further exacerbated in adolescence by pervasive consumer culture imagery that polarizes gender roles and portrays unrealistic standards of 'success'. We have yet to fully comprehend the damage that is being inflicted on younger generations as these images and expectations embed themselves deeper into children's psyches through social media. Daily, children are made keenly aware of how many 'likes' and 'follows' they are getting, pulling them further into a competitive race in which levels of fame and validation are relentlessly quantified.

Meanwhile, the World Health Organization (WHO) has reported that "Globally, more than 300 million people of all ages suffer from depression," which is now "the leading cause of disability worldwide."[11] Perhaps most alarming of all, in 2010 the WHO found that global rates of suicide had increased by 60 percent since World War II.[12]

Rarely are the systemic pressures behind these psychological costs recognized. Structural forces, for example, lead the average person in the US to move more than 11 times in their lives in pursuit of education and jobs. The continual cutting of ties to community and place clearly stunts the development of deep and lasting personal relationships – but since our hyper-competitive economy is treated as though it is 'normal', its consequences are largely ignored. Instead, there is a tendency to blame emotional problems on the individual or their own immediate circumstances.

At the same time, people in the North are often told that as privileged members of a 'first world' country they shouldn't complain. This rhetoric has blinded hundreds of millions of people in the wealthier countries to their deep spiritual impoverishment: modern life has stripped them of so many of the supports and relationships that are needed to be fully human and happy.

■ Environmental breakdown

Globalization is intensifying the already serious ecological consequences of industrialization by spreading a resource-intensive, growth-based consumer economy to every corner of the world.

Evidence of global environmental decline abounds. Topsoil is being rapidly lost through nutrient depletion and erosion from corporate agriculture. Whole tracts of irreplaceable forest are being decimated by the global timber, oil, and mining industries. The planet's diversity of plant and animal species is being lost at 100 to 1,000 times the natural rate of extinction, ranking the modern era as one of the planet's great extinction waves.[13] While terrestrial wildlife struggles to survive, the health of the world's oceans is also spiraling downwards due to plastic waste and other pollution, acidification and industrial fishing.

A 2014 study assessing the ecological footprint of nations highlights the impossibility of creating a global consumer economy in which everyone lives the American Dream: if everyone had the same per capita ecological footprint as an average American, we would need 5 Earths.[14]

Accelerating these trends through globalization is simply incompatible with the needs of the living world: our finite planet does not have the capacity to sustain an economic system based on ever-expanding consumption. Yet the premise of globalization is that more of the world's people – all of them, in fact – should be encouraged to enlist in this destructive system.

■ Increased CO_2 emissions

One of the clearest and most frightening effects of global economic activity is climate change – an impact made much worse by increased trade deregulation. Even the WTO admits that "more open trade would be likely to increase CO_2 emissions."[15] Much of this trade is needless. Food, for example, is routinely shipped halfway across the world to be processed, then shipped back and sold right where it started. Mexican calves – fed imported American corn – are exported to the United States to be butchered, then re-exported back to Mexico for sale.[16] Scottish prawns are sent to China to be shelled, while Canada's are sent to Iceland for the same reason.[17]

Most countries are also involved in 'redundant trade' – the simultaneous import and export of identical foods. In 2007, for instance, Britain imported 15,000 tons of chocolate-covered waffles, while exporting 14,000 tons.[18] In 2017, the US imported *and* exported nearly 1.5 million tons of beef, and nearly half a million tons of potatoes.[19] This kind of redundant trade is commonplace. It has nothing to do with meeting short-term shortages, and everything to do with maximizing profits.

Needless to say, unnecessary and wasteful transport adds massive amounts of CO_2 into the atmosphere. But emissions from the thousands of cargo-carrying ships and planes involved in global trade *do not appear in any nation's carbon accounting*. It is just another example of how trade and global growth are considered more important than anything else – even the climate.

The need for an ever-expanding energy supply for an ever-rowing global economy is creating an extractive mega-machine, with trillions of dollars spent on gas-fracking, mountaintop removal, tar sands mining, deep sea oil wells, nuclear power, geo-engineering, and more. With people in developing countries encouraged to emulate a Western, consumer lifestyle, the situation is rapidly worsening. Already, India is the third largest emitter of CO_2 in the world; its per capita emissions from energy use are projected to double from 2015 levels by 2030.[20]

■ Erosion of democracy

As decision-making becomes centralized into unelected, unaccountable bodies like the WTO, the IMF, and the European Commission, the influence of the individual steadily shrinks. This is true even in nominally democratic countries: people may still have the right to vote for national and local leaders, but as political parties from both the left and right embrace the wishes of corporate and banking interests, voting can become all but meaningless. This is especially true when ISDS rules mean that democratically-enacted laws and regulations can be overturned if they threaten corporate profits. And as corporate interests become ever richer thanks to globalization, they are able to increase their expenditures on lobbyists, campaign contributions, and political advertising – giving them still more influence over government decision-making. (See "Corporate rule", Chapter 9.)

■ Growing gap between the 'haves' and the 'have-nots'

Contrary to the commonplace slogan "a rising tide lifts all boats," global growth is actually widening the gap between rich and poor. The wealth of the eight richest people now equals that of the poorest half of the world's population – nearly 4 billion people – and the inequality is worsening.[21] Since the 1970s, income inequality has risen in nearly every industrialized country, but is particularly acute in the 'developing' world.[22] In China, for example, measures of inequality nearly doubled between 1980 and 2010. In a 2012 survey, Chinese people ranked it as the country's top social challenge, ahead of corruption and unemployment.[23] Since the end of the apartheid era, the wealth gap in South Africa has also increased, with shantytowns butted up against luxury, gated housing developments.[24]

■ Lack of resilience

Because globalization encourages countries to specialize their production, most now rely on imports for even basic domestic needs. Tied to a volatile global economy over which they have no control, they are vulnerable to the impacts of natural disasters, wars, disease, economic slumps – and of course, speculation – thousands of miles away.

■ Unhealthy urbanization

Globalization erodes rural economies, leading to a massive population shift from rural areas to the cities. This is particularly true in the South, where the global economy is steadily breaking down more self-reliant systems, leaving people little alternative but to migrate to cities whose populations are already exploding. In 2015, a staggering 1 billion people lived in urban slums – and the number grows every year.[25]

During the era of globalization, tens of millions of people have been evicted from their lands to make way for development projects undertaken in the name of 'progress' and economic growth. A 2015 report by the International Consortium of Investigative Journalists found that in the preceding decade alone, development projects funded by the World Bank "physically or economically displaced an estimated 3.4 million people, forcing them from their homes, taking their land or damaging their livelihoods."[26] This kind of displacement has been a primary driver of the growth of mega-slums.[27]

China offers an especially sobering case of forced urbanization: although it is now beginning to change, it was the country's official policy to move hundreds of millions of rural Chinese into urban areas, in the name of economic growth and development. According to a 2013 *New York Times* report, the goal of the government's modernization plan was "to fully integrate 70 percent of the country's population, or roughly 900 million people, into city living by 2025."[28] Some argue that this plan represents an unqualified improvement in the prospects for the great masses of Chinese peasants who are its targets, but it's unlikely that China's increasingly mechanized factories will be able to absorb such a massive influx of workers. Moreover, the urban jobs that are created are often highly exploitative. As the largest federation of labor unions in the United States, the AFL-CIO, has pointed out, China's primary economic advantage has rested on the government's "unremitting repression of workers' rights [and] the ruthless exploitation of an estimated 100 million rural migrants."[29]

In the most industrialized countries, too, jobs in the global economy are concentrated in sprawling metropolitan areas and their suburbs, while rural regions are systematically sapped of economic vitality.

In addition to a host of social problems, urbanization contributes to a substantial increase in resource use and pollution. Nearly every material need of urbanized populations must be shipped in from elsewhere, while the resulting waste – much of which could be put to use in a rural setting – becomes a highly concentrated source of pollution.

■ Loss of food security

There is a structural link between globalization and monoculture: global corporations are successful only if they can market identical products to a huge number of homogenized consumers. For the food system, this has meant a dramatic decrease in agricultural diversity, with thousands of local crop varieties abandoned for the relative few suited to monocultural production and long-distance transport. Overall, approximately 75 percent of the world's agricultural diversity was lost in the last century, a narrowing of the genetic base that puts food security at risk everywhere.[30]

A handful of corporations now control a growing proportion of the world's food supply.[31] Contrary to common belief, this means an inefficient, wasteful use of natural resources: large-scale monocultures are less productive per acre than smaller diversified farms (see Chapter 7). Corporate control also threatens access to food for many people, notably the residents of 'food deserts', who are surrounded by packaged junk food but lack access to nutritious, healthy, fresh food. Today, when the food supply is more tightly controlled by corporations than ever before, more than 800 million people are undernourished – even though more than enough food is produced to adequately feed everyone on the planet. [32]

■ The rise of conflict, violence and extremism

The rise of violence and civil disorder around the world is a predictable effect of an economic system that imposes monocultural stereotypes while simultaneously heightening economic insecurity. In the global South in particular, the loss of self-esteem, along with intense competition for increasingly scarce jobs, leads to deep social divisions. As people become trapped in a demoralizing system of cut-throat competition, an escalation in prejudice, racism, hostility towards immigrants, and tensions between ethnic groups is all but inevitable. Threats to one's identity from an advancing global monoculture can also lead people to cling to their traditions in an exaggerated fashion. As a result, all forms of religious fundamentalism are on the rise – Islamic, Christian, Jewish, Hindu and even Buddhist. Now, far-right authoritarianism has gained in popularity in country after country, turning populism into a divisive and destructive force. These issues deserve special attention, and will be looked into in detail in the next chapter.

4

THE RISE OF EXTREMISM

For those who care about peace, equality and the future of the planet, the political swing to the right over the past few years is deeply worrying. It has us asking ourselves, how did this happen? Why is right-wing authoritarianism on the rise, all over the world?

Based on what you've read so far, it will come as no surprise that I believe the answer centers on globalization. As we've seen, globalization is a process by which diverse local economies are replaced by a single, global system dominated – both politically and economically – by a relative handful of huge businesses and banks. But globalization goes deeper than politics and the economy. It has profoundly personal impacts, leaving people increasingly insecure on multiple fronts. And insecure people can be highly susceptible to false narratives that purport to explain their precarious situation.

From cooperation to conflict

Let me illustrate how this happened in Ladakh. In the traditional culture, work involved providing for the basic needs of the community – food, clothing, housing. Although there was little money in the typical Ladakhi household, there was no evidence of the kind of poverty one sees all over the so-called 'developing' world – where people are hungry or malnourished, and have neither adequate shelter nor clean drinking water. In fact, throughout Ladakh I was told regularly: "We are *tung-bos za-bos*", which means "we are self-sufficient, we have plenty to eat and drink".

During my early years in Ladakh, a remarkable degree of social harmony was evident; particularly noteworthy was the fact that the Buddhist majority and Muslim minority, who were economically interdependent, lived peacefully side-by-side. Of course there were problems, as there are in all human societies, but the harmony and *joie de vivre* I encountered was vastly different to what I'd known growing up in Europe.

Within a decade, however, there was a terrifying shift away from the traditional harmony, as Buddhists and Muslims began competing for scarce jobs and seeing one another as enemies. Ethnic and religious differences began to take on a divisive political dimension, causing bitterness and enmity on a scale previously unknown. Young Ladakhis, for whom religion had been just another part of daily life, took exaggerated steps to demonstrate their religious affiliation and devotion. Muslims began requiring their young daughters to cover their heads with scarves. Buddhists in the capital began broadcasting their prayers over loudspeakers, so as to compete with the Muslim prayer call. Religious ceremonies once celebrated by the whole community – Buddhist and Muslim alike – became instead occasions to flaunt one's wealth and strength.

In 1989, tensions between the two groups exploded into violence that took several lives. I heard mild-mannered Buddhist grandmothers, who, a few years earlier, were sipping tea with their Muslim neighbors and even celebrating each other's religious festivals, declare: "we have to kill the Muslims before they finish us off."

Outsiders attributed the conflict to old ethnic tensions flaring, but any such tensions had never led to group violence in 600 years of recorded history. As someone who lived there and spoke Ladakhi fluently, I had a unique perspective as both an outsider and insider, and it was obvious to me that there was a connection between the economic changes wrought by development and the sudden appearance of violent conflict.

The most noticeable changes in the economy centered on food and farming. Imported food, heavily subsidized by the Indian government, now sold at half the price of local products. As a result, food self-reliance was steadily replaced by dependence on the global food system, and many Ladakhis – the vast majority of whom were farmers – began to wonder if there was a future for them.

Changes in education also had a huge impact. In the past, Ladakhi children learned the skills needed to survive, even to prosper, in this difficult environment: they learned to grow food, to tend for animals, to build houses from local resources. But in the new Westernized schools, children were instead provided skills appropriate for an urban life within a globalized economy – a way of life in which almost every need is imported. The new schools taught almost nothing about the Ladakhi way of life; instead children were implicitly taught to look down on the traditional culture.

The locus of political and economic power changed as well. Traditionally, the household was the center of the economy, with most of the larger decisions taken at a village level. With the arrival of the global economy, economic and political power became centralized in the capital city, Leh, leaving villagers out of decisions that deeply affected their lives. Meanwhile, young men were being pulled out of their villages into Leh in search of paid jobs. Suddenly cut off from their village community and in cutthroat competition with hundreds of others for scarce jobs, their once-secure sense of identity was deeply eroded.

These changes were further amplified by an influx of foreign tourists, by the introduction of satellite television, and by a bombardment of advertising campaigns – all of which served to romanticize Western, urban culture, making the Ladakhis feel backward and stupid by contrast.

It was clear to me that the arrival of the global economy had created a pervasive sense of insecurity and disempowerment. On a practical level, the Ladakhis were becoming dependent on far-off manufacturers and centralized bureaucracies instead of each other. Psychologically, they had lost confidence in themselves and their culture. It is not hard to see how people so insecure and disempowered can turn to anger and extremism.

The speed and scale at which these changes took place in Ladakh was overwhelming, making the structural connection between globalization, insecurity and conflict very obvious. But it was also clear to me that the same process is underway around the world: the economic system has become a driver of fear, fundamentalism and political instability almost everywhere. And in both the global North and South, the enormous psychological and material insecurity fostered by globalization has greatly magnified the ability of demagogues to use fear and prejudice to manipulate public opinion.

To reverse this trend, neither a politics of identity, nor of conventional 'left' versus 'right', is sufficient. I believe that if we are to solve any of the major crises we face – including the rise of intolerance, fundamentalism, hyper-nationalism and authoritarianism – we need to fundamentally change the structural economic forces at the root of the problem. Those forces are the engines of globalization, and reversing that process is our best hope for peace and stability.

How has globalization led to a breakdown of democracy, to increasing fundamentalism and violence, and to the rise of far-right political leaders? To answer this question, it is vitally important that we see the broader connections that mainstream analyses generally ignore.

Globalization and insecurity

Many people associate globalization with international collaboration, travel and the spread of humanitarian values, but globalization is – more than anything else – an *economic* transformation, one that has been at the heart of neoliberal ideology and the corporate agenda since the end of World War II. In the global South, it's referred to as 'development'; in the global North, as 'progress'. But in both North and South the fundamental process is the same – the deregulation, centralization and privatization of business, finance and politics. These changes add to the bottom lines of multinational corporations and banks, but have a profoundly negative impact on society.

■ Job insecurity

With corporations ruling the global economy, even long-held jobs can disappear overnight. Many people live in constant fear of the unemployment line, while others cannot make ends meet even with a full-time job.

Although heightened job insecurity is a consequence of globalization, the remedy offered by policymakers almost never involves reversing corporate deregulation. In fact, "more of the same" is the most common prescription: more economic growth, fewer environmental regulations, fewer taxes, and more government support for high-tech. Although these are corporate-friendly responses, they are often packaged as efforts to protect the 'little guy' from big government. Many people whose lives have been upended by the current economic system embrace them, along with false narratives that blame immigrants or minorities – people who are victimized even more profoundly by the global economic system. Because almost no political leader is willing to point to the corporate-led global economy as the root cause of this and so many other problems, voices reflecting a right-wing, anti-government, and xenophobic perspective fill the gap.

■ Political insecurity

Deregulation is making global corporations and banks richer, but it is impoverishing governments. Their treasuries have been drained by the heavy subsidies and tax breaks handed out to attract big business, and further eroded by offshoring and the ability of multinationals to hide profits in countries with lower tax rates. Meanwhile, governments are left to cover all the externalities – the social and environmental problems that are the inevitable by-products of global growth. As a consequence, many people see their government leaders as inept – failures at running the nation's affairs – while the growing wealth and success of businesses suggests that the solution is to "run the country more like a business".

Increasingly distanced from the institutions that affect their lives and growing ever more insecure about their economic livelihoods, many people have become frustrated, angry, and disillusioned with the entire political system. Ignorant about the role of the global economy in the downward spiral of their communities, many people blame individual politicians or political parties – only to be disappointed when a change in office-holders or the party in power makes no difference for their community or their personal lives. Others vote for candidates who promise that further freeing big business by cutting 'red tape' will boost economic growth and create secure jobs. Because they don't see the bigger picture, they become increasingly susceptible to false claims and extremist views.

■ Psychological insecurity

As local and even national economies are undermined, the fabric of interdependence that holds communities together begins to fray. This not only leads to social fragmentation and isolation, it also unravels the safety net which ensures that the surrounding community can be relied upon for help in times of hardship.

At the same time, the global consumer culture is relentlessly expanding. People all over the world are targeted with advertising messages telling them: "you are not good enough as you are, but buying our product will make you better." With face-to-face relationships deteriorating and real-life role models replaced by artificial images of perfection in mass media and in the hyperbolic world of social media, unhealthy comparison runs rife.

Left insecure and marginalized by the new economy, people are highly vulnerable to prejudice. In the global South especially, the breakdown of communities and cultures is severing rich intergenerational relationships and uprooting identities. Those healthier identities are often replaced by destructive alternatives that reflect a desperate need for belonging. Ideological fundamentalism and extremism can seem to offer an explanation for worsening social and personal ills, as well as a radical solution. It can provide personal validation and meaning, solidarity and a sense of community – all essential human needs that have been undermined by globalization. In this way, the uprooting of the South's land-based populations has been the driver of much of the ethnic conflict, fundamentalism and radicalism seen in that part of the world.

Rural areas in the North have been similarly hollowed out by global economic forces. Family farms tied to the global food economy cannot compete with heavily subsidized agribusinesses, and their steady demise has decimated the local economies and communities they once supported. Young people who have grown up in these rural areas often see no future there: not only are jobs scarce, but – just as in Ladakh – the media and advertising tell them that urban life is 'cool', glamorous and exciting by contrast.

Ignorant about the destructive impacts of the corporate-led global economy, people are vulnerable to right-wing views. They can easily be persuaded to blame immigrants and minorities for their problems. And they often become anti-green and anti-left, believing that bloated government bureaucracy and expensive environmental and social protection measures are responsible for their economic woes. Many will vote in support of free trade and laissez-faire economics, believing that these policies will provide the prosperity they have been denied. Widespread lack of awareness about the bigger picture enables the far-right to gain strength.

To avoid further political instability, stalemate and chaos, we urgently need to spread the word about economic deregulation and its impacts on our communities and personal lives. It is only ignorance about this system that enables the pseudo-solutions of Trump, Brexit, Duterte and others to gain strength, even as the global economic system marches onwards, unfettered. Despite the fact that these right-wing political forces are often branded as 'anti-globalist', they are actually serving to strengthen global monopolies.[1]

5

LOCALIZATION
Getting from Here
to There

localization. *noun. 1. the removal of fiscal and other supports that currently favor giant transnational corporations and banks; 2. reducing dependence on export markets in favor of production for local needs (often confused with isolationism, protectionism, the elimination of trade.)*

If globalization is at the root of so many problems, it stands to reason that localization – a shift away from the global and towards the local – offers a systemic solution.

Localization is a process of economic decentralization that enables communities, regions, and nations to take more control over their own affairs. As we have seen, global banks and corporations are actively shaping our societies and our political institutions. Localization is a way of reversing this trend: instead of business determining the rules for society, citizens – through the democratic process – determine the rules for business.

Localization means shortening the distance between producers and consumers wherever possible, and striking a healthier balance between local and global markets. It does not mean that people in cold climates are denied oranges or avocados, but that their wheat, rice or milk – in short, their basic food needs – do not travel thousands of miles when they can be produced within a fifty-mile radius. Rather than ending all long-distance trade, steps towards localization reduce unnecessary transport while strengthening and diversifying economies at the community and national levels. The degree of diversification, the goods produced and the amount of trade will naturally vary from region to region.

If localization is thought of as an overnight change to a predetermined end point, it can seem impossible to achieve. The supply chains that bring food, clothing, energy, water, and every other need to huge, dense cities are incredibly complex – how can they be localized? But it's important to remember that, even now, the rules are being changed to facilitate a continuing acceleration towards the global. What localization means is simply shifting the direction of change so that it's towards the local instead of the global.

In places where local economic structures are still relatively sound – in the global South, for example – change can come fairly quickly. In places where the fabric of local community and economy has been almost completely unraveled, it may take longer and require more effort.

Shifting direction requires efforts on two very different levels. At the 'bottom up' grassroots level, millions of local and regional enterprises are already demonstrating that they can do a better job providing for basic needs than the handful of monopolies that currently dominate the economy. As we will see in the next chapter, these community-based projects reweave the social and economic fabric in ways that meet the needs of nature – both wild and human.

But in order for initiatives like these to spread more widely, localization also requires 'top down' policy change to reverse the structural forces that now promote the large and global. The aim of those policy shifts – and the goal of my organization – is to promote 'small scale on a large scale'. What follows are the policy shifts needed to make that vision real.

Trade treaties

A first priority is to insist that our governments get back to the same tables where they signed our rights away to global corporations. We need new treaties that will take back that power –

in part by requiring businesses to be place-based or localized, thereby making them more accountable to those they affect.

Instead of continuing to deregulate global trade, nations could work together on agreements that prioritize healthy local and national economies. The purpose of trade would no longer be to increase corporate profits and GDP, but to provide markets for surplus production and to obtain goods that cannot be produced domestically.

Many international networks of organizations and individuals have emerged to oppose the further deregulation of trade. In the days leading up to the 2014 parliamentary elections in Europe, more than 50 of these groups came together to draft an Alternative Trade Mandate, with 193 candidates pledging to support the Mandate's aims. These included proposals to "allow countries, regions and communities to regulate the production, distribution and consumption of goods and services; ... to prioritize local and regional food systems over global agricultural trade; ...[and] to hold corporations accountable for the social and environmental impacts of their operations."[1] More recently, a new coalition has emerged with the aim of eliminating the corporate-friendly Investor-State Dispute Settlement courts – a feature of most 'free trade' treaties. The network, StopISDS.org, is also pushing for a binding UN treaty to ensure that global corporations are held to account for their actions.[2]

Clearly, it will be difficult for any single nation to abruptly leave the 'free trade' regime: most national economies have been restructured over many decades to depend almost completely on trade. One possibility is a 'breakaway strategy', in which a small (and subsequently growing) group of nations collaborate to forge new trade treaties that allow the use of tariffs to limit the import of goods that can be produced locally. This 'protectionism' would not be targeted against fellow citizens in other countries; it would instead be a way of protecting jobs and local resources from the excessive power of transnational corporations and banks.

Such a group of breakaway nations would work co-operatively to reduce their trade dependence and to diversify their home economies, rather than continuing to specialize their production for the benefit of global capital. They could sign agreements to reduce levels of trade as their economies became increasingly self-sufficient – again, trading mainly in those things they can't produce for themselves.

Financial policies

Governments need to re-regulate the banking and financial system to curtail the unregulated flow of capital. At the same time, the local investment sector needs to be freed of outdated laws that make it almost impossible for people to invest in their communities through retirement funds and securities exchanges.

Shifts in lending practices are also needed. Currently, corporate banks discriminate against small businesses, charging them significantly higher interest rates for loans than they charge big firms. They also often require that small business owners personally guarantee their loans, and do not ask the same of directors of large businesses. And if government policies gave more support to community banks and credit unions, a greater number and variety of local businesses would thrive. In the United States, for example, small, localized financial institutions hold only about 11 percent of the banking assets, but they account for more than one-third of small business lending nationwide.[3]

Indicators of economic health

Decision-makers often point to rising levels of GDP as proof that their policies are working. They fail to acknowledge that GDP is woefully misleading as a measure of a country's well-being. GDP is simply a gross measure of market activity, of money changing hands. It doesn't distinguish between the desirable and the undesirable, between costs and gain. Increased expenditures on cancer, crime, car accidents and oil spills all lead to rising GDP, but any reasonable person would count these as symptoms of societal ill-health, rather than well-being.

Rising GDP may create a handful of billionaires, but in most countries the standard of living of the vast majority – including the middle class – is steadily declining. As I mentioned earlier, even governments are becoming poorer as their national GDPs grow.

What's more, GDP considers only those activities that involve monetary transactions, thereby leaving out the functions of family, community, and the environment. Thus, paying to send one's children to a day-care center adds to GDP, while care at home by members of the family does not. A forest cut down and turned into pulp adds to GDP, but a standing forest – crucial to the health of the biosphere – does not.

In the South, policies that focus on elevating GDP systematically lead to the breakdown of self-reliant economies that provide for people's needs with little use of cash. Through the process of 'development', healthy self-reliance is thus replaced by real poverty within the global economy.

A variety of alternatives to GDP are being developed and applied. The Genuine Progress Indicator (GPI) combines "critical economic, environmental and social factors into a single framework in order to give a more accurate picture of the progress – and the setbacks – we have made."[4] It has already been calculated for more than 20 countries and 20 US states.[5] In 2012, Vermont mandated that the state's GPI be calculated each year.[6]

Many people have also been inspired by the example of Bhutan, whose then-King articulated the concept of Gross National Happiness (GNH) as an alternative to GDP in 1972. In 2004, Bhutan helped launch an international movement to explore and promote the Gross National Happiness model. (Unfortunately, Bhutan's current government has begun distancing itself from the GNH concept.)[7]

Taxation

In almost every country, tax regulations systematically discriminate against small and medium-scale businesses. Small-scale production is usually labor-intensive, and heavy taxes are levied on labor through income taxes, social welfare taxes, payroll taxes, and more. Meanwhile, tax breaks (accelerated depreciation, investment allowances, tax credits, etc.) are given to the capital- and energy-intensive technologies used by large corporate producers. Reversing this bias in the tax system would help local economies and create more jobs by favoring people instead of machines.

Similarly, taxes on the energy used in production would discourage investment in robots and other energy-intensive technologies, help internalize some of the social and environmental costs of high-tech, and bring the cost of human labor closer to that of machines. Taxing fossil fuels in particular would result in a reduction in transport, an increase in regional production for local consumption, and a healthy diversification of the economy.

Decentralized renewable energy

Globally, direct subsidies for fossil fuel consumption are about double those given to renewable energy production.[8]

Reversing this imbalance would result in less pollution, more jobs, and long-term cost savings. For example, one study found that if New York State switched to renewables, it would result in a decline of around 4,000 pollution-related deaths annually. The state would save about $33 billion while creating permanent jobs in manufacturing, installation and maintenance.[9]

For all forms of energy, including renewables, decentralized power plants are preferable. Putting energy sources close to their end use lessens the need for long-distance transmission networks that reduce efficiency, consume resources, and gobble up land. Decentralized power sources also help to keep money from leaking out of local economies and thereby ensure greater decentralization of political power as well.

In the global South, where a large proportion of the population is still rural, large-scale energy plants – from coal and nuclear to huge hydroelectric dams – are geared towards the needs of urban areas and export-oriented production, thus promoting both urbanization and globalization. Supporting decentralized renewable energy infrastructures instead would strengthen villages, smaller towns and rural economies in general, thereby helping to halt unhealthy urbanization.

Local and national governments around the world are adopting new laws that are helping to spur the expansion of decentralized renewable energy, including tax incentives, subsidies, financing supports such as feed-in tariffs, and Renewable Portfolio Standards (policies that mandate specific renewable energy targets). Germany's Renewable Energy Act and feed-in tariff program is an outstanding policy example. In Canada, Ontario's Green Energy Act of 2009 contained a feed-in tariff with a bold 'buy local' provision that provided incentives to renewable energy projects that used local labor and manufacturing inputs. (Unfortunately, Ontario's local content requirement was abandoned in 2013 after a ruling that it violated WTO regulations.)

In the US, state-level Renewable Portfolio Standards have sparked a rapid expansion of solar and wind power, and could increase their impact by requiring jurisdictions to source a certain percentage of their electricity from decentralized and locally controlled renewable energy sources. Several states in the US have already adopted policies that promote neighborhood-scale community-owned solar energy projects, such as Colorado's Solar Gardens Act and Minnesota's Solar Energy Jobs Act.

Food and agriculture

Since food is something that every person on the planet needs every day, even small shifts in the way it is produced, transported and marketed can have dramatic effects. Direct farm subsidies in most countries heavily favor large-scale industrial agribusinesses. Funding for agricultural research is also heavily skewed in favor of biotechnology and chemical- and energy-intensive monoculture. According to one estimate, $49 billion is spent on food and farming research around the world each year, with less than 1 percent devoted to "knowledge, techniques and tools that are highly specific to, and in compliance with, organic standards."[10]

Shifting these expenditures towards those that encourage smaller-scale, diversified agriculture would help revitalize rural economies in both North and South, while promoting biodiversity, healthier soils, food security, balanced and diverse diets, and fresher food.

In the countries of the South, colonialism, development and globalization have led to a situation in which the best land is devoted to crops for Northern markets. Shifting the emphasis to diversified, low-input production for local consumption would not only improve economic stability, it would also reduce the gap between rich and poor, while eliminating much of the hunger that is now so endemic in the 'developing' parts of the world.

After decades of policy bias towards global food, local food is now gaining some regulatory support. In 2013, the government of Ontario, Canada passed a Local Food Act aimed at increasing access to local food, improving local food literacy, and providing tax credits for farmers who donate a portion of their produce to nearby food banks.[11] In the US, the Good Food Purchasing Program provides a framework for municipalities to create food procurement policies that support equitable food systems, based on local sourcing, nutrition, environmental sustainability, workers' rights, and animal welfare.[12] The program has been adopted by the San Francisco school system, by the cities of Los Angeles and Boston, and by Cook County, Illinois.[13] The most radical step of all has been taken in Vanuatu, an island nation in the South Pacific, where the Torba Province has banned all imports of foreign junk food in favor of an all-local and all-organic diet.[14]

Health and safety regulations

Regulations aimed at problems caused by large-scale production often create unfair burdens for small-scale enterprises. Battery-style chicken farms, for example, clearly need significant environmental and health regulations: their millions of genetically-identical, closely confined animals are highly prone to disease, their tons of concentrated effluent need to be safely disposed of, and the long-distance transport of processed poultry entails the risk of spoilage. Yet a small producer – such as a farmer with a dozen free-range chickens – is subject to essentially the same regulations, often raising costs to levels that make it impossible to remain in business. Those costs are more easily absorbed by large-scale producers, who can spread the cost of compliance over a far greater volume.

Such discriminatory regulations are widespread: they are decimating farm-based cheese producers in Europe, local apple cider producers in the US, and small-scale food businesses in many other countries.

In the US, most states have enacted 'cottage food laws' that relax the restrictions on small-scale production of jams, pickles and other preserved foods, allowing them to be processed and sold locally without the need for expensive commercial kitchens.[15] In 2017, Maine passed a law allowing municipalities to regulate their own local food systems – previously impossible due to federal and state regulations. Within one year, more than 40 towns had passed 'food sovereignty' ordinances that give citizens the right to "produce, process, sell, purchase, and consume local foods of their choosing," opening up countless business opportunities for small farmers and producers.[16]

Land use regulations

Local and regional land use rules could be amended to protect wild areas, open space and farmland from development. Political and financial support could be given to the various forms of land trusts that have been designed for this purpose. In some cases, local governments have used public money to buy the development rights to farmland, thereby simultaneously protecting the land from suburban sprawl while reducing financial pressure on farmers.

In urban areas, zoning regulations usually separate residential, business and manufacturing areas – a restriction necessitated by the needs and hazards of large-scale production and marketing. These could be changed to enable an integration of homes, small shops and small-scale production. Zoning regulations aimed at limiting high-density developments often end up prohibiting environmentally sound living arrangements like co-housing and ecovillages; rethinking these restrictions could facilitate community-based ways of living.

Infrastructure spending

High-speed motorways built with government funds indirectly subsidize corporate super-stores, hyper-markets, and shopping malls. Spending some of that money instead to build or improve spaces for public markets – such as those once found in virtually every European town and village – would enable local merchants and artisans with limited capital to sell their wares. This would enliven town centers while reducing car use, fossil fuel burning and pollution.

Creating and improving spaces for public meetings – from town halls to village squares – would encourage face-to-face exchanges between decision-makers and the public, serving both to enliven communities and to strengthen participatory democracy.

Global media

Television, the internet, and other mass media have received massive subsidies in the form of research and development, infrastructure build-out, educational training, and other direct and indirect support. In recent years, many national broadcasting companies have been taken over by global media empires. In the US, for instance, the Telecommunications Act of 1996 removed anti-monopoly provisions and deregulated the media sector, allowing large companies to acquire multiple media outlets, including television, radio, and internet sites. Such laws need to be rewritten to encourage a diversity of expression and ownership. Furthermore, communities and nations should have the right to restrict monocultural, violent, and commercial messages and images from bombarding their children.

Supporting facilities for regional entertainment – from community radio stations to live music and theater – would offer a healthy alternative to globalized media. The more people can engage in co-creating entertainment, such as dancing, singing and festivals, the more community bonds are strengthened. Children growing up with participatory entertainment, rather than being passively glued to a television screen or wireless device, have a greater sense of belonging to both place and their local culture.

Education

Schooling is increasingly geared towards the needs of corporations, which are presumed to be the future employers of today's children. In North and South, curricula are ever more standardized and technology-focused. In much of the developing world, formal education continues to be based on a colonial model: rote learning in the language of the colonial power; cultural and historical information coming from abroad; and training in skills relevant to the export economy rather than the local or regional economy. In most countries, this form of education filters out information about widespread social and economic problems in the North, leaving idealized myths about 'development' and the urbanized consumer culture intact.

Societies in both North and South would benefit enormously from a shift away from corporate-tailored curricula towards diverse forms of place-based learning. Rather than encouraging specialization for a competitive, corporate-led economy, education would be tailored to diverse environments, cultures and localized economies. Training in regional agriculture, architecture and appropriate technology would further decentralize production for basic needs. This does not imply that the flow of information from other cultures would be curtailed; cultural exchange would be an important part of the curriculum.

Healthcare

At present, investments in healthcare favor ever more technology for huge, centralized hospitals serving urban populations. The end result is that doctors and nurses have to serve more patients in less time, inevitably eroding the quality of care given to each patient. Spending the same money instead on a greater number of smaller local clinics – relying less on advanced technology and more on doctors and nurses, health education and holistic, preventive medicine – would bring healthcare to more people while boosting local economies.

There is increasing demand for less-invasive, integrative medicine, but at the moment heavy subsidies for corporate medicine mean that this is too expensive for the majority. Shifting subsidies to favor more natural healing methods would make them more widely available.

In the South, local economies and communities would greatly benefit if legal and financial support for healthcare were shifted towards localized and indigenous healing modalities that are affordable to the majority of the population. Modern medicine is an important addition to healthcare in developing countries. However, the healing traditions that currently provide most of the preventative care need support in order to survive.

Taking the initiative: Fair Tax Town

As things stand today, the playing field is steeply tilted in favor of global behemoths, rather than the smaller-scale businesses that would provide the foundation for localized, place-based economies. As we'll see in the next chapter, local initiatives continue to sprout from the grassroots all over the world, despite this disadvantage. But shifting policies to level the playing field would ensure that those efforts flourish and multiply.

One town in Wales is working to encourage such policy shifts by exposing the double standards of the tax system.[17] They are doing so by playing the same game as the corporate giants. It all began when Steven Lewis, owner of a small cafe in Crickhowell,

Wales, noticed that his business paid a hefty £31,000 in corporate income taxes in 2014, while Facebook only paid £4,327 tax on their £389 million revenue. Why should Facebook only pay 1/7 as much as my small business has to pay, Mr. Lewis asked himself.

It did not take him long to discover that, all over the world, multinational corporations take advantage of loopholes to avoid paying taxes, aided by trade treaties that allow operations to be sited in and revenues credited to whatever country has the lowest tax rate.

Needless to say, this gives multinational corporations a huge advantage over their small, locally-owned competitors. Threatened by the likes of Starbucks and Amazon, Steven Lewis and the small business owners of Crickhowell decided to take matters into their own hands. First, they attempted to incorporate their town and its businesses in offshore tax havens – a tactic favored by multinational corporations. The British tax authorities told them that neither Crickhowell nor its small businesses qualified.

Undeterred, the Crickhowell business owners set up a company to take advantage of the 'Dutch Sandwich' (a loophole created when a company is 'sandwiched' between the UK and a tax haven), and learned how to use intellectual property rules to reduce the profits they declare and, in turn, the taxes they pay.

Their company is called Fair Tax Town, and other towns across Britain have since signed on to join them. Their goal is not to avoid paying taxes, but to put Fair Tax Town in a stronger negotiating position with UK tax collectors: "The problem isn't with taxation", they say, "it's that there is one rule for the small guys and one for the big multinational companies."

Though this is not a lasting or systemic solution to the problems of economic globalization and deregulation, it is a clever way to shine a light on how the system is rigged against local businesses. One of Fair Tax Town's strategies is to shame corporate tax avoiders – and the governments that let them get away with it – through mainstream and social media campaigns. When sweet grandmothers stand in front of their family-owned bak-eries and say they'll cheat the tax system until Facebook stops doing the same, people may begin to listen.

6

GRASSROOTS INSPIRATION

Today, in every part of the world, thousands of local, bottom-up initiatives are already underway. Unlike actions to halt the global economic juggernaut, these small-scale steps require a slow pace and an intimate understanding of local contexts, and are best designed and implemented by local people themselves. If supported by the policy changes discussed in the previous chapter, such initiatives will, over time, foster a healthier environment, a return to cultural and biological diversity, and increased well-being worldwide.

The range of possibilities for local grassroots efforts is as diverse as the locales in which they take place. The following survey illustrates examples of steps being taken today, and is by no means exhaustive.

Local finance

Community banks and *credit unions* allow people to invest in their neighbors and their community, rather than in distant corporations. They also enable small businesses to obtain inexpensive start-up loans of the kind that banks typically offer only to large corporations. When the Occupy movement brought renewed attention to the unfair – even illegal – practices of big banks, US organizations launched a campaign encouraging people to move their money to smaller community institutions. In less than two months, more than 440,000 people switched their accounts away from the nation's Wall Street banks, removing nearly $5 billion from those institutions' hands.[1]

In Fortaleza, Brazil, residents of the impoverished Palmeira neighborhood founded their own community bank, governed and managed by local residents for local needs. Before it was launched, only 20 percent of residents' needs were purchased in the Palmeira district. Fifteen years later, 93 percent came from within the community – a resounding success in promoting the local economy.[2]

Local investing is also on the rise. From 2010 through 2018, Slow Money chapters in the US, Canada, Australia, and France moved $66 million into small farms and food businesses.[3] These groups are exploring other initiatives to localize financial instruments previously governed by big banks, including local stock exchanges, micro- and cooperative investment funds, and locally-invested pension funds.

Many progressive towns and organizations have created *local currencies* – a form of money that is only recognized by community members and local participating businesses – as a way to keep money from 'leaking' out of the local economy. More than 100 local currency initiatives are underway around the world, from Sand Dollars in California, to Bangla Pesa in Kenya, to Occitan in France.

Timebanks and Local Exchange Trading Systems (LETS) challenge the notion that money is the only instrument for facilitating meaningful exchanges of goods and services. Whether a piece of paper taped on the wall of a local café or an online database, these systems provide a medium for people to list the services or goods they have to offer and the amount they expect in return. Their accounts are credited for goods or services they provide to other members, and they can use those credits to purchase goods or services from anyone else in the local system.

"No money? No problem!" is the motto at the Cape Town Talent Exchange (CTTE), based in Cape Town, South Africa. More than 6,000 CTTE members trade goods and services by exchanging 'talents' rather than money. The goal is to maintain a balance between services rendered and received, with transparent online records encouraging people to give and receive evenly. The monthly currency-free Claremont Talent Market and the annual Learning Clan festival anchor and enliven the community. The CTTE model has now spread to 99 countries.[4]

Systems like these allow even people with little or no 'real' money to benefit from the circulation of credit within the local economy, and to strengthen their ties to the larger community. Over the years, however, we have found that local currencies, timebanks, and LETS initiatives work best in tandem with local food projects – on their own they are difficult to maintain.[5]

Local business

'Buy local' campaigns help local businesses survive, even when pitted against heavily subsidized corporate competitors. These campaigns not only help keep money from leaking out of the local economy, they also help educate people about the hidden costs – to the environment and to the community – of artificially cheaper, distantly produced goods. Grassroots organizations have emerged to oppose huge corporate marketing chains, especially in rural and small town economies. The rapid expansion of both McDonald's and Walmart has spawned citizen opposition in countries all over the world.[6] While these efforts often fall short, there have also been many successes, including in the Sierra Norte region of Mexico. (See "Resistance and renewal: Tosepan", below.)

Local business alliances enable small and medium businesses to network, support each other and build vitality in local economies. In North America, BALLE (Business Alliance for Local Living Economies) encompasses more than 80 networks representing around 30,000 independent businesses. They host conferences, provide guidance for starting and running a successful small business, and share inspiration.

Local business **loyalty card networks** are also emerging. These are similar to the loyalty cards frequently offered by big box stores, but can only be redeemed for discounts on local purchases. In Portland, Oregon, the Supportland network includes dozens of local businesses and is looking into expanding their model to other towns and states.

Local energy

Many towns around the world have invested in *community-owned decentralized energy* installations. 'Solar gardens', where local households and businesses sign up for a share of electricity from an offsite solar array, are becoming popular in the USA.[7] Many organizations, such as Cooperative Energy Futures in Minnesota and Evergreen Cooperative in Ohio, focus on creating local employment opportunities and on empowering renters and low-income households to reap the benefits of cooperatively-owned clean energy.[8]

In many parts of the world, citizens are working to mobilize their local governments to reclaim ownership and control over their power systems from non-local investor-owned utilities (IOUs) through '*re-municipalization*'. In 2013, residents of Hamburg, Germany voted to reclaim their electricity grid from the Swedish energy giant Vattenfall, enabling the city to undertake a more ambitious transition towards local renewable energy.[9] In a movement led by the youth group New Era Colorado, citizens of Boulder, Colorado voted in 2011 to give their municipality the authority to reclaim its energy systems from coal-powered giant Xcel Energy.[10] Eight years later, the city is now acquiring Xcel's assets and establishing its own municipal electricity service.[11]

Others adopt *Community Choice Aggregation* policies that allow cities and counties to create new local electricity providers alongside IOUs. As of 2018, 20 counties and cities in California operate on Community Choice models, bringing renewable energy to more than 2.5 million people at a lower cost than the IOUs, using the electrical infrastructure already in place.[12] The sector is growing rapidly all over the country, reversing the privatization trend that began in the 1980s.

Microgrids – interconnected networks of distributed energy producers and users – are also becoming more common, especially in the developing world. ME SOLshare in Bangladesh, for example, builds peer-to-peer solar energy networks, enabling owners of solar panels to link up with nearby homes and businesses to trade electricity. Many microgrid systems like these are built by communities that do not yet have access to electricity and prefer to develop localized, resilient, renewable systems from the start rather than follow the standard path of centralized energy development. Others, like Brooklyn Microgrid in New York City, are focused on creating local self-sufficient electricity systems even though power from the main grid is already available.

After Hurricane Maria struck Puerto Rico in the fall of 2017, parts of the island were left without power for 11 months. It was an unprecedented disaster, but also a unique opportunity for residents to seize local control in the wake of the US government's neglect. Resilient Power Puerto Rico, founded after Maria's devastation, brought human-scale energy to hard-hit parts of the island by distributing solar-electric power kits and guiding their installation. Their goal is for each neighborhood to achieve energy sovereignty, and to end the island's dependence on the top-down fossil fuel economy. Originally a stopgap response to a climate-caused disaster, it is evolving into a long-term effort to give communities control of their own energy future.[13]

The benefits of these decentralized projects extend beyond their use of non-polluting renewable energy sources. Because the power is produced right where it is needed, there is no need to expand transmission infrastructures. Residents have greater control over their energy costs and are not beholden to distant energy companies. And local investors can receive financial returns in times of surplus production – creating positive value for people and the planet.

Local food and farming

In the last decade or so, the local food movement has emerged as one of the most successful grassroots efforts worldwide. *Com-*

munity supported agriculture (CSA) programs, in which consumers link up directly with nearby farmers and receive a portion of the harvest throughout the year, have helped small-scale diversified farms to thrive in growing numbers. In the US the number of CSAs has grown from just two in 1986 to more than 7,300 in 2015.[14] They provide small farmers with a steady and reliable market and up-front advances for the season's expenses, while giving consumers produce that is fresher and healthier than supermarket fare. Many farms offer the opportunity to help with the harvest; some offer whole-diet shares with seasonal grains, vegetables, fruit, proteins, and herbs. All of them connect consumers with the farmers who grow their food, and help to build community.

Farmers' markets have similar benefits. The number of farmers' markets in the US grew from 1,755 in 1994 to over 8,600 in 2018,[15] and in the UK the number increased by 800 between 1996 and 2014.[16] Many of these markets are enormous community events featuring a maze of stalls bursting with fresh produce, homemade goods and artisan crafts, with live music and the aroma of freshly prepared food drifting through the air. But even if it's just a single farmer setting up shop in a neighborhood park, markets are a great place to connect with others who want to help shift the food system towards the local.

A related trend is the growing demand for *local organic food*, which has increased exponentially: the area of land under organic cultivation in Europe, for example, doubled between 2004 and 2017.[17] Even though large-scale producers and export-oriented marketers have tapped into this burgeoning segment of the food market, organic methods are most conducive to small-scale, diversified production for local consumption. Four Root Farm in Connecticut, for instance, grows nearly 200 varieties of vegetables and more than 300 varieties of cut flowers organically on just 5 acres of land.[18] This diversity creates resilience against pest and disease outbreaks and creates a richer, healthier experience for the farmers and customers alike.

Permaculture – an amalgam of 'permanent agriculture' and 'permanent culture' – is a way of growing food in human-designed ecosystems that mimic the diversity and resilience of natural ecosystems. Because permaculture focuses on whole-systems design, it provides a conceptual framework for designing not just food systems, but entire sustainable societies. Thousands of permaculture projects, large and small, are underway worldwide. One of the most successful is the Chikukwa permaculture initiative in eastern Zimbabwe. Over a period of two decades, the project has transformed six villages from a state of chronic food insecurity and severe environmental degradation to one of food sufficiency, community self-reliance, and ecological regeneration – all by consciously redesigning their food production systems with permaculture principles in mind.

Farmland trusts protect arable land from development, thereby enabling small farmers to afford to stay on the land and keeping farmland affordable for the next generation. In the US, where almost 31 million acres of agricultural land were lost to development between 1992 and 2012, state and national farmland trusts are working to protect what remains and to encourage sustainable management of existing farm and ranch lands.[19]

In both the global North and South, many *young farmers* are reversing the decades-long trend of rural exodus by going back to the land. Most of them are interested in healthier food and ecologically-sound methods of producing it. But because they must compete with developers and big agribusinesses, one of their biggest challenges is securing affordable land. The Agrarian Trust in the US helps address this and other issues by providing information and resources, land and job listings, and legal advice to young people transitioning back to the land. The Trust also owns farmland that it leases to young organic farmers, thereby lowering the cost of entry into the agricultural economy.[20]

In the US, the National Young Farmers Coalition has attracted more than 140,000 members and supporters since it was founded in 2010.[21] La Via Campesina, a worldwide coalition that connects 200 million members in 81 countries, has an active youth chapter.[22]

At their inaugural meeting in 2011, the group declared: "As youth all over the world have been systematically displaced from the countryside, our food system has lost its integrity and legitimacy, polluting the land, poisoning our people and robbing us of our rural cultures. We, the young peasants and farmers of La Via Campesina, who are building ecological alternatives on our farms and in our countryside, are living in resistance to this system."[23]

Community media

Community media outlets give ordinary citizens a voice and keep people informed about what is happening locally. In an era of corporate-controlled media, these outlets can be a means of ensuring that dissenting views can still be heard. They are also powerful tools for strengthening community bonds, maintaining local culture, and bringing people together to address local problems.

Community radio stations exist in many towns both in North and South – from Haryana, India to Istanbul, Turkey, and from Berkeley, California to Byron Bay, Australia. These stations do not rely on corporate advertising: instead they are supported directly by the communities they serve. They report on local issues neglected by larger media outlets, inform the public about upcoming events, and provide an opportunity for diverse local opinions to be heard. Although most of the programming is locally-derived, many also provide an outlet for alternative syndicated programs that are disseminated internationally.

For the most part, television has been taken over by large corporate interests, but in a few places *independent channels* still exist. In the US, Link TV is supported by viewer donations and specializes in broadcasting hard-hitting documentaries from around the world. While the internet is known as a place where disparate views can be heard, attacks on net neutrality threaten to give the biggest players an unfair advantage over smaller information providers. In response, many groups have banded together in an effort to maintain free and equal access to the web.

In the US and many other countries, most people are dependent on a handful of corporate-owned internet service providers, such as Comcast, Charter Communications, AT&T and CenturyLink. However, a *community-owned broadband* movement has recently emerged to increase communities' control over their internet services. As of 2018, more than 750 municipalities across the US have built their own broadband networks as a way to guarantee their access to more affordable and reliable internet services, and to keep dollars circulating in their local economies.[24]

Place-based education

It's critically important to decouple the concept of education – developing the skills and character to thrive and meaningfully contribute to the world – from the practice of mainstream schooling. I saw in Ladakh how healthy it is for children of different ages to play and learn together: the older ones help those who are younger, and the young ones learn from and find role models among older children.

When children are segregated by age in classrooms, they lose this natural dimension of human interaction, and cooperation gives way to competition. Forcing them to be still and quiet in a windowless room for hours at a time is also profoundly unnatural. Add social media into that mix and the result is a recipe for discontent, poor self-esteem, and aggressive behavior.

Thankfully, many *alternative schools*, worlds apart from the regimented methods and curricula of mainstream schooling, are recognizing the need for children to play freely, to explore outdoors, to interact with people of different ages, and to nurture the curiosity that comes naturally to children. Two of the most widespread models are the Steiner Schools (also known as Waldorf Schools) and Montessori Schools – elements of which are beginning to be incorporated in some public school systems. *Homeschooling*, in which children are taught by parents or members of the community, is also gaining in popularity. So is *unschooling*, which allows children to follow their innate desire to learn about topics that interest them.

With a growing awareness of what has been described as

'nature deficit disorder', an increasing number of schools use wild and agricultural places as an educational setting. In *Forest Schools*, for example, children spend their entire day outdoors, in the process becoming experts in local plant and mushroom identification. They also learn how to observe, interact with, and integrate into the gentle rhythm of their natural surroundings: "I don't have ADHD when I'm in the woods," said one 14-year-old forest school student.[25] The concept originated in Wisconsin in 1927, and has since spread to Scandinavia and the UK, where it has become very popular. In Vermont, the ROOTS School (Reclaiming Our Origins through Traditional Skills) is one of a growing number of schools offering classes in wilderness self-reliance for young people and adults.

In the global South, more and more people are recognizing the culture-homogenizing impacts of Western-style schooling. In India, Shikshantar – the People's Institute for Rethinking Education and Development – is working to transform education so that it respects local traditions and promotes self-reliance.[26] Everyone is welcome to learn and teach at Shikshantar – from young kids raised on the street, to academics, to village elders. The institute's workshops, study groups and activities vary by the day, but the sharing of food, co-creation of music, and meditation are regular features.

Shikshantar is also connected to the hand-built and renewably-powered Swaraj University, which offers young people from around India the opportunity to embark on a two-year learning journey. These *koji* ('seekers') are encouraged to pursue ideas and crafts that may be unconnected to commercial 'success', and that are absent from conventional higher education in India.

Healthcare

In recent years, there has been a tremendous surge of interest in *traditional and complementary medicine* – herbal remedies, homeopathy, bodywork, relaxation techniques and more. These gentler approaches, with an emphasis on prevention, are part of a return to more human-scale systems of healthcare, and are even attracting interest from conventional medical doctors. It is, of course, important to continue providing the emergency and life-saving care that allopathic medicine excels at. But a localized system of healthcare, emphasizing the whole person and their broader living context, is just as important. As the director of the Center for Sustainable Medicine in Vermont puts it, "real medicine must benefit the whole system – our communities, both human and natural. There is no need to separate the processes of healing ourselves, the environment, and our communities."[27]

Pax Herbals in Nigeria is pioneering this kind of whole-person community-based healthcare approach, centered on organically grown herbal medicines. Its Herbarium project is documenting indigenous healing wisdom, and has collected more than 5,000 species of medicinal plants in Nigeria. It is now conducting scientific research on the plants, with the aim of integrating African healing traditions into an evidence-based medicine system. With its hospital, research laboratories, and farms, the center has created hundreds of jobs and student internships in a rural area. This has slowed the migration of local youth to cities while preserving local ecosystems and biodiversity – yet another example of localization as a solution-multiplier.

Community-building

All over the industrialized world, people are building residential communities as an alternative to the isolation, competitiveness, and pollution that are so pervasive in modern societies. Many of these *intentional communities* rely on renewable energy, natural building techniques, and on-site food production, and actively develop cooperative local economies in their surrounding areas.

Ranging in size from just a few households to many hundreds, *ecovillages* are among the most popular, successful, and diverse kinds of intentional communities. The Global Ecovillage Network connects thousands of communities across the world through virtual and real-world alliances.[28] The communities are as diverse as the locales they are built in, and range from formerly abandoned villages reclaimed by youth, to urban apartment buildings with shared common spaces and meals, to income-sharing cooperatives connected to the land.

Popular in North America and Europe, *Transition Towns* consist of community groups in small towns and larger urban centers that have committed to transitioning away from a globalized, carbon-intensive economy. The Transition network now encompasses thousands of groups that meet regularly to set up projects in different sectors of the local economy: food, energy, local commerce, the arts, transport, healthcare, and so on. Popular Transition Town projects include community gardens and repair cafés – free meeting places with tools and skilled volunteers to help people learn to mend their broken possessions.[29]

The *community rights movement* helps communities reclaim local democratic decision-making power. One of the founding organizations of this movement in North America is the Community Environmental Legal Defense Fund (CELDF). To date, CELDF has helped nearly 200 locales establish "community rights ordinances" protecting them from such activities as fracking and the planting of GMO crops.[30] The Landworkers' Alliance in the UK, a democratic union and member of La Via Campesina, increases the political decision-making power of farmers and workers on small agroecological farms through political trainings, advocacy, campaigning, and more.[31]

Taken together, these grassroots steps – and many thousands like them in communities around the world – are a testament to human ingenuity and goodwill. They are the most visible and inspiring pieces of a worldwide localization movement that is gathering strength day by day. Coupled with efforts to resist further globalization, these steps towards renewal show that another way is, in fact, possible. Every one of these initiatives is incredibly valuable, but I'm convinced that the most important involve local food – a subject that I will explore in greater detail in the next chapter. But first, let's look at an example of resistance and renewal in more detail.

Resistance and renewal: Tosepan

Since the mid-1980s, Mexico has been a poster child for globalization, with grim consequences that are by now familiar. And yet, throughout Mexico, there is a florescence of inspiring resistance and alternatives, some long-established, some only now springing up.

In the southern state of Puebla, local communities defending their territories and livelihoods are confronting corporate-state development projects, including mining, gas fracking, centralized electrical grid infrastructure, big dams, and big box stores. Government concessions have been granted in Puebla for 11 mines and 14 hydroelectric projects, along with petroleum development (including fracking).[32]

But a fierce backlash across the state has successfully blocked many of these projects. In the Sierra Norte, the resistance has been particularly spirited and effective, causing a number of hydropower projects to be suspended, and a planned Walmart (under its Mexican subsidiary name, Bodega Aurrerá) to be scuppered.

Some of the most effective resistance has emanated from a network of cooperatives called Tosepan that has been working in the region for 40 years, building up a parallel solidarity economy among largely Nahua and Tutunaku indigenous communities, encompassing some 35,000 members across 430 villages.

Tosepan was instrumental in encouraging a citizens' plebiscite to reject a proposed Walmart/Bodega Aurrerá store in the town of Cuetzalan in 2010, by using arguments about the economic, cultural and environmental harms it would cause[33] – and the fact that Walmart's promised 60 low-quality jobs would come at the cost of 500 local businesses, and put at risk the entire solidarity economy built up by Tosepan and others.[34] The significance of this victory cannot be overstated in a country where Walmart has been steadily expanding: 1 in 5 Walmart stores worldwide are in Mexico.[35]

Tosepan is comprised of three civil associations and eight cooperatives, which together cover basic needs. Their projects include:

- agroecological farming of staples like corn, beans and vegetables, as well as coffee, pepper, and sugarcane, both for sale (primarily to local markets) and for the community's subsistence;
- natural building using local resources like bamboo and adobe;
- small-scale technologies like water harvesting, solar dehydrators, and ecological cookstoves;
- healthcare, focusing on prevention and traditional herbal remedies;
- decentralized renewable energy with a goal of total energy sovereignty; and
- local finance to support the functioning of the entire ecosystem of cooperatives

There has been a special emphasis on food sovereignty in Tosepan, with the goal of meeting local needs first. One of their many agricultural projects has been to bring back the native bee, *Scaptotrigona mexicana*. The bees' honey, propolis, and wax have many medicinal properties, while the pollen is rich in proteins. The cooperative also makes products like shampoos, soaps and creams from the honey and wax.

Since 2001, Tosepan's members have also been involved in organic coffee production based on highly diversified, biologically rich agroecological "gardens of coffee" that are possibly the most diversified coffee farms in Mexico. A single hectare may contain over 200 species of plants, with multiple ecological and social functions and values.

The ethos guiding Tosepan's work is explained by one of Tosepan's members, María Luisa Albores: "Our cooperative model is based in values of a cosmovision or form of life that closely coincides with the social and solidarity economy which values life, people, the land, plants, and animals. From this vision we have constructed the mode of life of Tosepan... The sense of belonging and permanence in our territory gives us identity...in the face of the onslaught and displacements of the capitalist system. Here we are and will continue with dignity, on foot walking in our land, which is sacred."[36]

7

LOCAL FOOD FOR OUR FUTURE

Food is something that everyone, everywhere, needs every day. For this reason, even small changes in how food is produced, distributed and marketed can have a huge impact. That makes the food system one of the most important places to begin shifting direction.

Local Futures has promoted numerous local food initiatives over the past 40 years. Such initiatives are among the most important lifeboats of resilience – alternative structures that will help keep our communities afloat during the upheavals to come.

When it comes to ecologically sound ways of producing food, the world is full of good news. Small farmers, environmentalists, academic researchers and food and farming activists have developed and documented best practices in agroecology, holistic resource management, permaculture, regenerative agriculture systems, and other methods that can alleviate or perhaps even reverse the global food system's worst impacts: biodiversity loss, energy depletion, toxic pollution, food insecurity and massive carbon emissions.

These inspiring methods have two things in common: they involve smaller-scale farms adapted to local conditions, and they depend more on human attention and care than on energy and technology. In other words, they are the opposite of industrial monocultures – huge farms that grow just one crop.

Biased towards monoculture

To significantly reduce the many negative impacts of the food system, these small-scale initiatives need to spread all over the world. Unfortunately, this transformation of farming has not yet received any significant support from policymakers. That's because the food system is inextricably linked to a government-supported economic system that, for decades, has been fundamentally biased against the kinds of changes we need. In the global South, in fact, existing sustainable farming systems are being steadily dismantled in favor of export-oriented monocultures. This is happening despite the fact that peasant farmers provide food to more than 70% of the global population, using less than 25% of the land, water and energy resources.[1]

Put simply, economic policies almost everywhere continue to systematically promote ever-larger scale, toxic monocultural production. As noted throughout this book, those policies include massive subsidies for globally traded commodities, direct and hidden subsidies for global transport infrastructures and fossil fuels, and 'free trade' policies that pry open food markets to global agribusinesses. At the same time, health and safety regulations usually place an unfair burden on small producers for local markets.

These policies provide a huge competitive advantage to large monocultural producers and corporate processors and marketers – which is one reason why industrially produced food that has been shipped from the other side of the world is often less expensive than food from the farm next door.

The environmental costs of this bias are huge. Monocultures rely heavily on chemical inputs – fertilizers, herbicides, fungicides and pesticides – which pollute the immediate environment, put wildlife at risk and, through nutrient runoff, create 'dead zones' in waters hundreds or thousands of miles away.[2] Monocultures also depend heavily on fossil fuels to run large-scale equipment and to transport raw and processed foods across the world, making them a major contributor to greenhouse gas emissions. In fact, scientists estimate the greenhouse gas toll of the global food system at one-third of total emissions.[3]

Among the most hideous effects of industrial monoculture is the way animals are treated. 'Factory farms' and concentrated animal feeding operations (CAFOs) crowd animals together in often-filthy, prison-like conditions. In meat production, the goal is simply to fatten the animals as quickly as possible, and then to transport and kill them at the lowest possible cost. The cruelty to animals is cause for growing concern around the world. So is the fact that the meat, milk and eggs produced by this system are prone to contamination, leading to hazards to the food supply. In 2018, for example, more than 25 million pounds of meat products were recalled in the US for possible salmonella, listeria, E. coli, and other forms of contamination.[4]

Industrial-scale production has social and economic costs as well. In the industrialized world, smaller producers can't survive; their land is amalgamated into the holdings of ever-larger industrial farms in the process decimating rural and small town economies and threatening public health through pesticides, herbicides, and toxic byproducts from CAFOs.[5] In the global South, the same forces pull people off the land by the hundreds of millions – leading to poverty, rapidly swelling urban slums and waves of economic refugees.[6] As described in Chapter 4, uprooted small farmers easily spiral into unemployment, poverty, resentment and anger.

There are also risks to food security. With global economic policies homogenizing the world's food supply, the 7,000 species of plants used as food crops in the past have been reduced to 150 commercially important crops, with rice, wheat and maize accounting for 60 percent of the global food supply.[7] Varieties within those few crops have been chosen for their responsiveness to chemical fertilizers, pesticides and irrigation water, and for their ability to withstand long-distance transport. A similar calculus is applied to livestock and poultry breeds, which are skewed toward those that can grow rapidly with inputs of grain and antibiotics in confined animal feeding operations.[8] The loss of diversity even extends to the size and shape of food products:

harvesting machinery, transport systems and supermarket chains all require standardization.

The end result is that more than half of the world's food varieties have been lost over the past century; in the US, the loss is more than 90 percent.[9] The global food system rests on a dangerously narrow base: without the genetic variety that creates resilience, the food system is vulnerable to catastrophic losses from disease and the disruptions of a changing climate.

The benefits of local food

The solution to these problems involves more than a commitment to ecological models of food production: it also requires a commitment to local food economies. Localization systematically alleviates a number of environmental problems inherent in the global food system, by:

- reducing the distance that food travels, thereby lessening the energy needed for transport, as well as the attendant greenhouse gas emissions;
- minimizing the need for packaging, processing and refrigeration (which all but disappear when producers sell direct to consumers) thus reducing waste and energy use;
- eliminating monocultures, as farms producing for local or regional markets have an incentive to diversify their production, which makes organic production more feasible, in turn reducing the toxic load on surrounding ecosystems;
- providing more niches for wildlife throughout diversified organic farms; and
- supporting the principle of diversity on which ecological farming – and life itself – is based, by favoring production methods that are best suited to particular climates, soils and resources.

Local food provides many other benefits. Studies all over the world have shown that small farms – the mainstay of local food systems – produce far more food per acre than large-scale monocultures.[10] If we're concerned about how the planet's growing human population will be fed in the coming years, we should pressure to end the subsidies that prop up industrial monocultures, and shift them towards smaller-scale farms.

Local food creates more jobs as well. The farms that produce for local and regional markets require more human intelligence, care and work than monocultures, thus providing more employment opportunities. In the global South, in particular, a commitment to local food would stem the pressures that are driving millions of farmers off the land.

Local food is also good for rural and small-town economies, not only providing more on-farm employment, but supporting the many local businesses on which farmers depend.

Food security is also strengthened because varieties are chosen based on their suitability to diverse locales, not the demands of supermarket chains or the requirements of long-distance transport. This place-based selection of plant varieties and livestock breeds strengthens overall agricultural biodiversity.

Local food is also healthier. Since it doesn't need to travel so far, local food is far fresher than global food; and since it doesn't rely on monocultural production, it can be more easily produced without toxic chemicals that can contaminate food.

The small diversified farms that supply local food systems also eliminate the cruelty to animals that is so typical of CAFOs and factory farms. Animals are usually not confined and spend much of their time outside in conditions not so different from their wild counterparts.

Making the shift

For more than a generation, now, the message to farmers has been to "get big or get out" of farming, and many of the farmers who remain have tailored their methods to what makes short-term economic sense within a deeply flawed system. To avoid bankrupting those farmers, the shift from global to local would need to take place with care, providing incentives for farmers to diversify their production, reduce their reliance on chemical inputs and fossil fuel energy, and seek markets closer to home.

Those incentives would go hand-in-hand with reductions in subsidies for the industrial food system.

As pointed out in Chapter 5, some local and regional governments have taken steps to support local food. But national governments, for the most part, are still directly and indirectly subsidizing global food, and providing the deregulatory framework global agribusinesses require. Far more pressure needs to be put on policymakers at all levels if there is to be any hope of eliminating the damage done by the global food system. A crucial first step is to raise awareness of the costs of the current system, and the multiple benefits of local food. No matter how many studies demonstrate the virtues of alternative ways of producing and distributing food, the destructive global food system is unlikely to change unless there is heavy pressure from the grassroots to change the entire system.

Fortunately, there are already many models proving that local economies centered on food sovereignty can provide for peoples' needs better than the global, corporate economy can. Here are a few examples:

Pine Island Farm

The labyrinth of global food trade has no shortage of absurd stories. Take, for example, the 3,000 frozen goats shipped from Australia to Burlington, Vermont each year. [11]

They were brought in to feed the region's growing community of 'New Americans' – refugees who came to the US to flee violence, repression or ethnic cleansing in their countries of origin. Many were farmers or herders before they were driven from their homes, and share a preference for goat meat and vegetable varieties that were simply not available in New England.

Pine Island Community Farm was founded in 2013 to address their needs by locally growing a cornucopia of foods from around the planet. The farm is a partnership between The Association of Africans Living in Vermont and The Vermont Land Trust, which offered a 230-acre property to the project with a no-cost lease for five years. Shortly after that, Chuda Dhaurali, a refugee from Bhutan, became the project's pilot goat farmer. Theogène Mahoro from Rwanda joined in, and now leads chicken operations at the farm. Now, more than 60 New American families use the farm's garden plots both for home and commercial gardening.

Pine Island not only offers New Americans the opportunity to access locally grown, affordable, culturally relevant foods – it also gives these new arrivals a way to connect with land and community in ways similar to what they left behind. The farm is a gathering place and event venue for traditional celebrations from all over the world, complete with a spit large enough to roast a whole goat.

The project also links the New Americans to the broader community, providing a friendly bridge between groups that might otherwise view one another with mistrust. Long-established Vermonters buy free-range chickens at the farm, feed their post-holiday Christmas trees to the farm's goats, and volunteer in exchange for a discount at the city's cooperative grocery store. In defiance of the anti-immigrant sentiments making headlines in much of the world recently, Pine Island shows the power of local food systems to unite diverse people in the shared dream of a healthy, community-based way of life.

Mouans-Sartoux Farm to School Program

Imagine if your town made it a priority to feed your children fresh, organic produce at school every day. In the small town of Mouans-Sartoux, in southeast France, residents did just that. [12] The town council set a goal that 100% of the food served in its three public school cafeterias should be local and organic. It changed its procurement policies, but there was not enough local produce available for the school meals. So in 2010 the town hired its first farmer, bought equipment, and officially launched its own municipal farm.

By 2015, the farm was producing 85% of the organic vegetables used in local school meals, covering 1,400 meals per day. The program reduces food waste by coordinating cafeteria menus with seasonally available produce, and by processing and storing harvested produce during school holidays. It also engages the children in growing their own food, sells vegetables at a discount to low-income residents, and donates surpluses to the local food bank. Much better than the usual mid-day serving of hamburgers, french fries, pesticide residues and obesity!

Pun Pun Center for Self-Reliance

"When I was a kid, everything was fun and easy," Jon Jandai explains, recalling his childhood in a village in eastern Thailand. "But when the TV came, many people came to the village. They said, 'you are poor...you need to go to Bangkok to pursue success.'"[13]

So he did. After living seven years in the city, working ceaselessly, sleeping in a tiny, crowded room, eating noodles every day with barely enough money to scrape by, disillusioned by the disconnect between university teachings and the basic processes needed to sustain life, he returned to his village and to the simpler life he had cherished in his youth. His family of six, working two months per year in their rice fields, harvested more than eight times the amount of rice they would eat for the whole year. After digging a fishpond and planting a garden, Jon had more than enough fish and vegetables for his family's needs, while tending the garden for just 15 minutes per day. They sold their surplus food, and he built a debt-free earthen house for himself in three months working only two hours a day. He stopped worrying about fashionable clothing and other status symbols. With more free time, he became better attuned to his mind and body, and learned to address illness and health imbalances by relying on his own intuition. Life became easy and fun again.

In 2003, he and Peggy Reents from the USA decided to create a learning center to share these insights, and the Pun Pun Center for Self-Reliance – an organic farm, intentional community, and a center for seed-saving and sustainable living – was born.[14] The land they bought, north of Chiang Mai, was seriously degraded as it had previously been used for mono-cropping corn. They figured that if they, with almost no money, could turn the land into an abundant, self-sufficient farm, learning center, and home, then people coming there to learn would have to believe that anything was possible.

Today, the crops at Pun Pun are diverse and thriving. The land yields rice, many local perennial edibles, herbs, vegetables and varieties of fruit; they also have fishponds and laying hens. Roughly 15 people live on the farm, and hundreds of guests and workshop attendees also pass through every year to learn about organic gardening, natural building, and the use of appropriate technologies – like simple solar systems for heating water, and homemade charcoal for water filtration.

Members of the Pun Pun community also run two restaurants in Chiang Mai city, where they serve local, organic, GMO-free food – much of it grown at the farm. The mission of both restaurants is to highlight the value of the diverse traditional seed varieties grown and saved at Pun Pun. As Jon explains, "Seed is food, and food is life. If there is no seed, no life. No seed, no freedom. No seed, no happiness."[15]

A local food economy never stands in isolation; it is connected to other threads of the social fabric in ways that make entire communities healthier and more resilient. Jon sums up his journey back to the land, to seeds, to life, freedom, and happiness: "We were taught how to make life complicated and hard all the time...we were taught to disconnect ourselves, to be independent, so that we can rely on money only, and don't need to rely on each other. But now, to be happy, we need to connect to ourselves again, to connect to other people, to connect our minds and bodies together again."[16]

8

COUNTERING
THE OBJECTIONS

Whenever I speak publically about localization, audiences raise a number of concerns. Here are some of the most common:

■ **Isn't globalization necessary to relieve poverty in the 'developing' world?**
There is a widespread belief that people in the countries of the South need Northern markets to lift themselves out of poverty, and that a greater degree of self-reliance in the North would therefore undermine economies in the less-developed world. But a gradual shift towards smaller scale and more localized production would actually benefit both North and South, and facilitate meaningful work and fuller employment everywhere. At present, the globalized economy requires the South to send a large portion of its natural resources to the North as raw materials. Its best agricultural land must be devoted to growing food, fiber, and even flowers for the North, and a good deal of the South's labor is employed in the cheap manufacture of goods for Northern markets. Rather than further impoverishing the South, localizing would allow the South to keep more of its own resources, labor and production for itself. For example, a 2014 study showed that 550 million people in Asia, Africa, and Oceania could be fed from land that has been taken over by foreign governments and corporations – mostly for exported food and biofuel crops.[1]

■ **Doesn't localization lead to isolationism at a time when we need global cooperation?**

There is no doubt that we need international collaboration to solve our global problems. Governments and grassroots groups alike need to exchange information across borders, and to push for binding agreements to reduce pollution, poverty and conflict. Unfortunately, many people believe that *economic* globalization is necessary for this type of collaboration. But as I hope is clear by now, globalization is leading to more conflict and competition, and exacerbating the very social and environmental problems we most urgently need to address. Forging international alliances that focus on scaling down the power of multinational corporations – enabling societies to set the rules for business, rather than the other way around – is the most strategic way forward.

■ **Isn't localization a form of social engineering?**

While shifting towards local economies would require policy changes that impact people's lives, those impacts would be minor compared to the unprecedented scale of social engineering in today's 'jobless growth' society. Vast stretches of the planet and entire economies are being shaped to conform to the needs of global growth, while people around the world are being encouraged to abandon their languages, their foods and their dress for a standardized monoculture. And in India, China, and other countries, policymakers explicitly call for moving hundreds of millions of people from villages to urban centers.

Rather than a centralized prescription from above, localization creates opportunities for diverse communities to define and pursue their own future.

■ **Aren't there too many people for the majority to live on the land?**

Because most of the industrialized world is largely urbanized, it can seem that life on the land is a thing of the past. What is too easily forgotten is that nearly half of the world's people today – mostly in the less-developed world – are still rural. Ignoring them

– speaking as if people are urbanized as part of the human condition – is a dangerous misconception that helps fuel the whole process of urbanization. It is thus considered utopian to suggest a ruralization of America's or Europe's population, while China's plan to move 250 million people off the land and into cities within a 12-year timespan hardly elicited surprise.[2]

Even in the North, rural communities are being steadily dismantled, their populations pushed into spreading suburbanized megalopolises where the vast majority of available jobs are centralized. In the United States, less than 20 percent of people still live in rural areas; farmers comprise less than one percent of the total population, and the number continues to decline.[3]

It is impossible to offer that model to the rest of the world, where large proportions of the population still earn their living as farmers.

■ Aren't cities more efficient?

Even though people physically occupy a smaller unit of land per capita in cities, urban centers around the world are extremely resource-intensive. The large-scale, centralized systems they require are almost always more stressful to the environment than small-scale, diversified, locally-adapted systems.[4] Food, water, building materials and energy for cities all come from great distances via vast energy-consuming infrastructures; their concentrated wastes must be hauled away in trucks and barges, or incinerated at great cost to the environment. In their glass and steel towers with windows that never open, even air to breathe must be provided by fans and pumps, usually powered by non-renewable energy.

From the most affluent sections of Paris to the slums of Calcutta, urban populations depend on increasing amounts of packaging and transport for their food, so that every pound of food consumed is accompanied by still more petroleum consumption, as well as significant amounts of pollution and waste.

The problem is not the city per se: smaller towns and cities that maintain a balance with their rural surroundings are able to maintain both ecological and cultural vitality. But urbanization today does not foster healthy urban-rural relationships. It is a continuous process of centralization – of aggregating populations in sprawling metropolises, where they must rely on industrial products to meet their most basic needs. This process may create 'efficiencies' for profit-seeking corporations, but from an ecological and resource perspective it is neither sustainable nor efficient.

■ Don't most people prefer to live in urban areas?

It's often said that people everywhere are more attracted to city life, and that therefore the urban tide cannot be turned. However we need to keep in mind that throughout modern history, there has been tremendous pressure – both psychological and structural – to pull people into cities. At the dawn of the globalizing economy, these pressures included force and coercion. Later on, the pressures involved a continuous romanticization of modern city life, with urban modernity portrayed as an escape from the supposed brutishness, ignorance, and hopelessness of rural life.

Today, similar psychological pressures come from films, television programs and advertising, from schoolbooks and classrooms, even from the internet. Almost all of our avenues for gaining knowledge have been profoundly affected by the assumption that urbanization, economic growth and technological progress are the only means of improving people's lives.

In this latest stage of globalization, industrial economies have been transformed into information or service economies, but the urbanizing pressures continue unabated. Mainstream media continues to depict urban life as the locus of cutting-edge culture, while jobs and economic opportunities are concentrated in high-tech urban areas and their surrounding suburbs.

None of this is inevitable. If steps were taken to provide resources and employment opportunities in smaller towns and rural areas, there is little doubt that these places would thrive both economically and culturally, and would begin attracting residents. Throughout the industrialized world, increasing numbers of young people are actively trying to move back to the land, as seen in the permaculture, ecovillage, and new farmers movements.

■ Don't we need industrial agriculture to feed the world?

Supporters of industrialized agriculture would have us believe that farming today is more productive than ever – and that to feed the world we have to further intensify and globalize our food system. Yet, despite all our pesticides, fertilizers, genetic modification and high-tech processing systems, a tragically large proportion of the global population still goes to bed hungry every night. This is because the goal of the globalized system is not to provide adequate, nutritious food for people, but to provide profits for large agribusinesses, supermarket chains and other transnational food corporations.

If we really want to feed the world, we need to begin localize our food systems as soon as possible. As noted in a 2013 report from the United Nations Committee on Trade and Development, "relying on international markets to meet staple food demand, while specializing in the production and export of 'lucrative' cash crops, has recently failed to deliver its desired results."[5] The 60 international experts who contributed to the report recommended an approach to food production that supports small farmers, agricultural diversity and self-reliance. Not only would this help alleviate poverty and hunger, they argued, it would also produce more food overall. That's because small-scale, diversified farms have a higher total output per unit of land than large-scale monocultures, based on studies carried out all over the world. In Kenya, for example, researchers found that if all domestic farms had the same productivity as the smallest ones, the country's agricultural output would double.[6] Unfortunately, Kenyan farms are still being taken over by foreign corporations, amalgamated and turned into vast monocultures for export.

■ Isn't 'fair trade' the solution?

Any international trade needs to be fair. Today's fair trade standards can offer guidance, but the primary emphasis should be on producing for local needs rather than for export. Even under fair trade conditions, dependence on foreign markets means a precarious existence for producers. Countries in both North and South would be far better off if they were allowed to protect and conserve their natural resources, and prioritize support for national and local businesses that provide for local needs.

■ Doesn't localization mean going back to the past?
In modern discourse the past is often looked down upon as something to be left behind as we surge towards a gleaming, high-tech future. The localization movement doesn't advocate returning to an idealized past, but it does draw important lessons from both the history of land-based cultures and the history of their demise.

This is an important topic that we will revisit later in the book. But first – having gained familiarity with both globalized and localized economic systems – it's time to look more deeply at the structural drivers and impacts of globalization.

9

GLOBALIZATION REVISITED

This book argues that the most serious problems we face – environmental, social, economic and even psychological – all stem from the same root cause: an out-of-control global economy. It may seem overly simplistic to see globalization as structurally connected to so many problems, but that's because the huge scale of the economy makes it very difficult to see those links. Even government leaders and corporate CEOs can be unaware of the impact their decisions have on the other side of the world. The same has become true of most of us: the distances between producers and consumers have grown so wide that it has become all but impossible to make ethical choices. A fish served in a California restaurant may have been caught illegally on a Thai fishing vessel manned by slaves. A t-shirt bought in Germany may have been sewn in a Bangladeshi sweatshop, where workers labored in unsafe conditions for starvation wages. The rising consumption levels of India's middle class may be contributing to climate chaos many thousands of miles away. In other words, it's like having arms that have grown so long we cannot see what our hands are doing.

This chapter will look at the drivers of globalization and its structural impacts, and explain how the economic system has become so destructive.

Trade deregulation

One of the earliest modern trade agreements, the General Agreement on Tariffs and Trade (GATT), was established in the aftermath of World War II with the explicit purpose of reducing tariffs and other so-called 'barriers to trade'. Starting in the 1990s the number of trade agreements began to increase sharply. The year 1994 was a watershed: the North American Free Trade Agreement (NAFTA) came into force, and the World Trade Organization (WTO), the supranational institution that now regulates global trade, was created. Since then, literally thousands of regional and bilateral trade and investment agreements have been ratified.

What all of these treaties have in common is that they give corporations and foreign investors the freedom to move in and out of national economies in search of subsidies, cheap labor and resources, low taxes, and lax environmental and social protection measures.

Deregulatory treaties also allow corporations and banks to be proactive in gutting regulatory policies they don't like. They can do so by challenging those policies as barriers to trade or foreign investment. As I pointed out earlier, many 'free trade' treaties include investor-state dispute settlement (ISDS) clauses that give corporations the right to sue governments if they believe that regulations will reduce their expected profits.

The number of ISDS cases has risen dramatically since the mid-1990s when the first modern 'free trade' treaties were signed into law. Through July 2017, the number of disputes totaled 817, with 69 new cases introduced in 2016 alone. Of the cases that have been concluded, 25 percent were decided in favor of investors, 33 percent in favor of States, and the remainder settled or discontinued.[1] Recent emblematic investor-state dispute cases include:[2]

■ Corporations versus public health: Philip Morris v. Uruguay and Australia

US tobacco giant Philip Morris sued Uruguay and Australia over their anti-smoking laws. The company argued that warning labels on cigarette packs and plain packaging prevented it from effectively displaying its trademark, causing a substantial loss of market share.

■ Corporations versus environmental protection: Vattenfall v. Germany

In 2012, Swedish energy giant Vattenfall launched an investor-state lawsuit against Germany, seeking €3.7 billion in compensation for lost profits related to two of its nuclear power plants. The case followed the German government's decision to phase out nuclear energy after the Fukushima nuclear disaster.

■ Corporations versus government response to financial crisis: utilities v. Argentina

When Argentina froze utility rates and devalued its currency in response to its 2001-2002 financial crisis, it was hit by over 40 lawsuits from corporations like CMS Energy (US) and the water companies Suez and Vivendi (France). By the end of 2008, awards against the country totaled more than US$1 billion.

■ Corporations versus environmental protection: Lone Pine v. Canada

On the basis of the North American Free Trade Agreement (NAFTA), US company Lone Pine Resources Inc. demanded US$250 million in compensation from Canada. The 'crime'? The province of Quebec placed a moratorium on fracking, based on concerns about the technology's environmental risks.

■ Corporations versus public health: Achmea v. Slovakia

At the end of 2012, Slovakia awarded €22 million in compensation to Dutch insurer Achmea (formerly Eureko), because the Slovak government had reversed the privatization policies of the previous administration and required health insurers to operate on a not-for-profit basis.

■ Corporations versus democratic process: Gabriel Resources v. Romania

The Romanian parliament refused to pass a law that would have permitted a Canadian mining corporation to operate an open-pit gold mine near the village of Rosia Montana. The company then sued Romania for US$4.4 billion – the 'lost profits' it expected from the mine.

Because of international trade treaties signed and ratified over the last several decades, most nations are now bound up in agreements that force them to acquiesce to the demands of big corporations and banks, or to engage in costly legal battles that take place in secretive, corporate-friendly arbitration tribunals outside of their own domestic courts – a threat to fair and transparent governance, and a threat to democracy itself.

Exponential growth in global trade

Trade is an activity that people and nations have engaged in for millennia. But in the past, long-distance trade was a secondary concern for most societies: the primary economic goal was meeting people's needs using the resources available within relatively short distances. Only once essential needs had been met locally did questions of trading surplus production with outsiders arise.

Today, however, international trade has come to be pursued as an end in itself. This modern emphasis can be traced to political economist David Ricardo's theory of comparative advantage, published in 1817. He argued that nations are better off if they specialize their production in areas where they excel, and then trade their surpluses for goods they need but no longer produce.[3] Although the supposed goal is increased efficiency, the result is a highly *inefficient* and wasteful system. But since most of the social and environmental costs are 'externalized' – shifted to taxpayers or the environment – the theory's shortcomings are not immediately apparent.[4]

In the mistaken belief that trade is always good and that more trade is always better, governments make massive investments in trade-based infrastructures, sign on to trade treaties that open their economies to outside investment, and scrap laws and regulations designed to protect national and local businesses, jobs and resources.

Whole economies are becoming dependent on trade, affecting every sphere of life. The impact on food – one of the only products that people everywhere need on a daily basis – is particularly revealing. Today, one can find apples shipped from New Zealand in apple-growing regions of Europe and North America. Shoppers on the Citrus Coast of Spain will find lemons from Argentina on supermarket shelves, while perfectly good local lemons are left to rot.[5] In Mongolia – a country with ten times as many milk-producing animals as people – shops carry more European dairy products than local ones.[6]

In an era of runaway climate change and dwindling fossil fuels, this kind of wasteful trade – which greatly overshadows the efforts of well-meaning individuals to reduce their personal carbon footprints – is little short of madness. What are the benefits of transporting food or any other basic commodity such distances, when they can be (and indeed for centuries have been) produced locally? How can these arrangements be described as economically 'efficient'? As we will see, this excessive trade benefits massive corporations and speculators at the expense of the majority. And it is not efficiency, but a wide range of subsidies and ignored costs, that makes it all possible.

Direct subsidies

Proponents of globalization point to the lower cost of many globally-traded goods as proof that economic efficiency is at work. However, a close look at the way the global economy is subsidized undercuts this argument. Not only do governments promote trade through international treaties, they do so by handing out hundreds of billions of dollars in direct subsidies to the trading sector of their economies through tax breaks, market access programs, production subsidies, loan guarantees, and more. Here are just a few examples of the countless direct subsidies benefiting corporations:

- In the US, the Market Access Program provides about $200 million annually to companies and trade associations to expand international markets for products ranging from Welch's grape juice and Blue Diamond almonds to beer, liquor, candy bars and pet foods.[7]

- The Export-Import Bank, a US government agency, provides loans and loan guarantees to international buyers of US goods and services. Of the $6.9 billion in direct loans made by the agency in 2013, 81 percent was for purchases from just five firms, including Bechtel and General Electric; 65 percent of the bank's $12.2 billion in loan guarantees supported exports from just one company, Boeing.[8]

- Governments often provide direct production-related subsidies for goods destined for export markets. According to the Environmental Working Group, the US government doled out an estimated $205 billion from 1995 to 2017 to support a narrow range of commodity crops (corn, cotton, rice, wheat and soybeans) that were grown on large monocultural farms and sent to distant national or international markets. While most of these subsidies, 77 percent, went to the largest 10 percent of industrial agribusinesses, the majority of small-scale diversified farms – which primarily focus on meeting local needs – received no subsidies at all.[9] The EU's agricultural subsidy program, part of the Common Agricultural Policy, has also favored large industrial farms and export-oriented agribusinesses over small local producers.

- Chapter 2 described some multi-billion dollar subsidies to individual big businesses. The watchdog group Good Jobs First tallied 393 examples of such 'megadeal' subsidies, in which local and state governments in the US provided $50 million or more per company to locate in their area. The list of recipients included many familiar transnational corporations, including Exxon-Mobil, Royal Dutch Shell, Citigroup,

Goldman Sachs, Walt Disney, General Electric, Dow Chemical, Amazon, Apple, Intel and Samsung.[10] Walmart has received more than one billion dollars in state economic development subsidies in the US alone.[11]

- During tough times, governments often bend over backwards to support big businesses. Following the financial crisis of 2008, giant corporations (especially large financial institutions) received substantial government support in the form of cheap loan bailouts, while community banks and small businesses were left to flounder. All told, the US Federal Reserve provided an estimated $4.7 to $29 trillion to bail out banks across the country, including some of the largest ones – JP Morgan Chase, Citigroup and Goldman Sachs – even though these companies played a direct role in destabilizing the financial system in the first place.[12]

Indirect subsidies

Governments also provide *indirect* or *hidden* subsidies to big businesses. By reducing the cost of long distance transport, for example, fossil fuel subsidies indirectly subsidize global trade, and help to prop up the energy-intensive system of mass production for mass consumption that globalization has spread around the world.

Indirect subsidies also include government investments in the infrastructures that a trade-based economy requires. These taxpayer-supported infrastructures include:

- Long-distance transport networks – multi-lane highways and motorway networks, shipping terminals, airports, high-speed rail, container facilities, export processing zones, etc.;
- Energy infrastructures – large, centralized electric power plants (including nuclear power stations and huge hydroelectric dams), petroleum facilities, gas and tar oil pipelines, etc.;
- High-speed communications and information networks – satellites, mobile telephone networks, television, radio, and the internet;

- Research and development institutions – facilities that develop labor-displacing technologies for industry and agriculture, and technologies to expand and modernize the physical infrastructures supporting the global economy.

Though small businesses and the general public also use much of this infrastructure, transnational corporations and their global supply chains benefit disproportionately from it. It's therefore not surprising that, in 2014, leaders from the twenty largest economies in the world launched the G20 Global Infrastructure Initiative, pledging trillions of dollars to help fund this massive expansion of infrastructure – an announcement that alarmed many ecologists but delighted the corporations involved in global trade.[13]

An additional kind of hidden subsidy involves the negative impacts associated with economic activity – the health effects of pollution, for example, or the damage caused by climate change. These costs are almost never subtracted from corporate bottom lines; instead, these 'externalized' costs are paid by society and the natural world, amounting to hidden subsidies that artificially inflate corporate profits. Commenting on a report showing that industry is consuming the planet's natural capital (forests, soils, fisheries, mangroves, ecosystem services, etc.) at a rate of nearly $7.3 trillion per year, journalist Jeff Spross noted that "Much of the global economy, in other words, is a giant Ponzi scheme that is (temporarily) viable *only* because markets fail to account for the value and use of the natural ecology – on which civilization depends for its crops, water, air, its very livelihood."[14]

Because of this system of direct and indirect subsidies, the price of goods transported halfway around the world can seem artificially cheap in comparison to goods produced next door. When I lived in Spain, for example, I found that garlic transported all the way from China was half the price of locally grown garlic. In large measure that was because neither the pollution involved in its transport nor the cost of the required transport infrastructure were reflected in its price. These subsidies, with their ignored social and environmental costs, distort the prices in the marketplace almost beyond comprehension. Consider the following examples:

- The fossil fuel energy required by large-scale producers and international trade is heavily subsidized. According to an IMF study, global fossil fuel subsidies amounted to a staggering $5.3 trillion per year – the equivalent of $10 million every *minute*.[15]

- According to one analysis, worldwide infrastructure investment amounted to roughly $36 trillion from 1995 to 2013, much of which was publicly funded. The same report concluded that an estimated $57 trillion in infrastructure investment will be required between 2013 and 2030 to sustain global economic growth, including investments for roads, rail, ports, airports, water, power and telecommunications.[16]

- A 2010 study conducted for the UN estimated the combined environmental externalities of the world's 3,000 biggest companies at $2.2 trillion in 2008, "a figure bigger than the national economies of all but seven countries in the world that year."[17]

- A 2014 study estimated that the total ignored ecological cost of human activity falls between $4.3 and $20.2 trillion per year! For comparison, the total annual value of the US economy is around $16-17 trillion, while the world economy is roughly $70 trillion per year. According to the same study, the benefits that humanity derives from the world's natural ecosystems – grasslands, marshes, coral reefs, forests, and the like – amount to an estimated $143 trillion each year.[18]

- A 2013 study on climate change – perhaps the largest externality of all – found that "just 90 entities are responsible for extracting most of the fossil fuels that have been burned over the past 150 years. These 'carbon majors' include 50 investor-owned companies, such as Texaco and Exxon-Mobil, 31 state-owned companies, such as Saudi Aramco and Pemex, and nine government-run industries in the former Soviet Union, China and other countries. Emissions from burning these fuels total nearly two-thirds of all the carbon that has been emitted into the atmosphere during the industrial era." [19]

- In a sense, today's globalized economy has been subsidized by the countries of the South for the past 500 years, at great expense to their own cultures, their land and their economies. The centuries-long dominance of the Western industrial countries could never have arisen without prolonged access to the South's raw materials, markets and labor – including slave labor. Although the true cost of the slave trade is incalculable, calls for reparations have ranged from tens to hundreds of trillions of dollars.[20]

Deregulating big banks and financial institutions

Financial deregulation had already begun by the 1970s in many countries, but accelerated dramatically in 1999, when 70 WTO member countries, representing more than 95 percent of the world's financial services activity, agreed to "eliminate or relax current restrictions on foreign involvement in the financial sector, including banking, securities and insurance."[21] Provisions for deregulating financial services have been incorporated into hundreds of bilateral and regional trade agreements that have been signed since then.

As investors became increasingly free to move capital around the world in search of higher profit, financial hubs like New York City, London, Frankfurt and Singapore relaxed their regulatory oversight still further, in order to attract finance capital. New markets and complicated financial instruments were created, contributing to an explosive growth of profits for banks and financial institutions, but to heightened instability of the entire financial system.

Not surprisingly, deregulation has led to an increase in the frequency and severity of financial crises. With massive flows of capital able to move quickly in and out of countries at the click of a button, entire economies can be quickly destabilized, creating surges of unemployment and economic hardship. Volatile capital flows contributed to economic crises in Mexico (1994), Turkey (1994 and 2001), Southeast Asia (1997), Argentina (2001), and the global financial crisis of 2008. And as economies have become more interconnected, financial crises have become more contagious, spreading quickly from one country to another.

A further reason for the volatility of the global financial system is that so much of the money circulating within it is 'phantom wealth' – defined by author David Korten as "financial assets that appear or disappear as if by magic as a result of accounting entries and the inflation of asset bubbles unrelated to the creation of anything of real value or utility."[22]

Much of this phantom wealth has been created by deregulated banks through debt pyramids, in which asset bubbles create phantom collateral that can be used to support further borrowing. Banks are required to hold only a small fraction of deposits in their reserves, using the rest for loans and speculative ventures. During the last few decades of financial deregulation, banking reserve requirements have been lowered to such an extent that about 97 percent of the money circulating in the economy today – the digital pulses that correspond to billions and trillions of dollars – is backed by nothing but debt.[23] Every time a bank issues a loan, money has been 'created' – money that must be paid back to the bank with interest. Private banks have, in effect, been given a license to print money.

Rather than being used to meet the real needs of communities, most of this steadily expanding supply of money is being created for no other purpose than to obtain the highest and quickest returns possible. Much of the money is used for purely speculative purposes: to make still more money.

A proliferation of new financial instruments emerged in the context of deepening financial integration and deregulation. One of the most common is the derivative, whose value is based on still other financial instruments, such as real estate loans, commodities futures, stock market indices or currency valuations.

Derivatives gained popular attention because of their role in the 2008 financial crisis: mortgage-backed securities, collateralized debt obligations, and credit default swaps were all implicated.

The lessons of 2008 seem to have been forgotten. The global value of derivatives was estimated at $595 trillion as of 2018, or more than six times the entire world's annual GDP.[24] The enormously complex and shadowy derivatives market remains largely unregulated and continues to make the entire system highly unstable, which is why Warren Buffett has referred to these instruments as "financial weapons of mass destruction".[25]

The leveraging of debt into huge speculative trades on financial and stock markets – another cause of the 2008 global financial meltdown – remains a central feature of the global economy. According to a 2015 McKinsey Global Institute report, "Seven years after the bursting of a global credit bubble resulted in the worst financial crisis since the Great Depression, debt continues to grow. In fact, rather than reducing indebtedness, or deleveraging, all major economies today have higher levels of borrowing relative to GDP than they did in 2007. Global debt in these years has grown by $57 trillion."[26] The problem has continued to worsen: in the first quarter of 2018 alone, debt increased by $8 trillion, bringing the total to an unfathomable $247 trillion.[27]

Financial deregulation has also contributed to the dramatic increase in inequality, both within and between countries. Massive speculative bets on exchange rates can cause national currency values to crash overnight – enriching a handful of investors but causing real hardship for the majority. In commodities markets as well, a high proportion of trades are speculative, with no actual physical goods being traded. But the impacts of speculation are all too real: bets on agricultural commodities can cause their prices to collapse, driving farmers into bankruptcy, or to spike, causing millions of people to go hungry. The latter happened in 2008, when food riots broke out in many developing countries.[28]

Despite a brief hiatus following the 2008 financial crisis, stock markets, financial sector profits and Wall Street bonuses have soared, while wages for ordinary workers have remained stagnant at 1970s levels. As two scholars recently concluded about the US, "the rise of finance is one of the driving forces behind growing income inequality and the concentration of income at the very top."[29]

Meanwhile, the system of ever-expanding interest-bearing debt creates a structural imperative for further economic growth to forestall the next financial crisis – even though the ecological destruction wrought by endless growth now imperils the biosphere itself. This is clearly a system run amok.

Debt, structural adjustment and austerity

The process of development requires energy, transport, and other infrastructures geared towards export-oriented industry and agriculture. Developing countries must borrow tremendous amounts of capital to build up this infrastructure, and if prices for their exports decline, they may be unable to repay their loans. They are then pressured to undertake 'structural adjustment' programs to enhance their international 'competitiveness' – the requirement for further loans. This means cutting back on social spending, opening up the country to outside investment, and providing still more funding for trade-based infrastructures.

World Bank and IMF lending to Southern countries is typically made conditional on such programs, and the vast majority of these countries have been subjected to them. The continual loan repayments, for which the interest alone can equal a large percentage of the country's annual budget, require surpluses that can only be generated by trading away natural resources or a significant portion of national output.

Even the 'rich' countries of the North are enmeshed in debt and dependence, thanks to globalization. Transnational corporations are increasingly able to bargain with governments for lower tax rates and higher subsidies by threatening to offshore their operations. At the same time, governments must find money in their tight budgets to provide support for the growing ranks of the unemployed, to retrain displaced workers, to mend the unraveling social fabric, and to clean up the despoiled environments left behind by mobile corporations. Forced to go hat-in-hand to international lenders, countries can easily find themselves on a downward spiral, with interest payments consuming an increasing proportion of the national budget. It's no wonder that so many governments today are struggling to stay afloat, while global corporations and banks are flush with cash.

Spain, Portugal, Greece, and several other countries have experienced these struggles in recent years. Not even the United States is immune: during the debt ceiling crisis of 2011, the country lost its top-tier credit rating as politicians wrangled over further expansions of government borrowing. Only a last-minute deal to raise the debt ceiling prevented the US from defaulting on its loans. The situation was nearly repeated again two years later. By the end of 2018, US national debt had reached nearly $22 trillion.[30]

For smaller countries, even a small fraction of that debt can be crippling. To mollify creditors, governments implement austerity measures that usually lead to higher unemployment, cuts to critical social programs, and massive protests. Their situation is unlikely to improve when they sign up for the only 'solution' offered: more debt and less autonomy.[31]

Corporate rule

Economic globalization has given big businesses unprecedented influence over policymaking. Governments naively support what they think of as 'their' transnationals, even though corporations today demonstrate no loyalty to place. Some of this benevolence towards large corporations may stem from the 're-volving door' between government and big business. For example, the chair of the US Federal Communications Commission (FCC) from 2001-2005 is now the head of the cable industry's primary lobbying group – a position that the 2013-2016 FCC chair once held.[32] Such blatant conflicts of interest are commonplace: a 2011 study revealed that 400 former US legislators and

5,400 former congressional staffers had become lobbyists over the previous decade.[33]

Governments claim they are representing the interests of their citizens when they negotiate trade treaties. The reality, however, is that the representatives around the negotiating table are essentially working on behalf of transnational corporations. Negotiations for the Trans-Pacific Partnership (TPP) were held in secret behind closed doors, with the public left to depend on leaked documents for information about the proposed terms; meanwhile, over 600 corporate 'trade advisors' had seats at the negotiating tables from the beginning.[34]

Campaign contributions also play a role. During the US Senate debate over 'fast-tracking' the TPP, for example, members of the US Business Coalition for TPP – comprising many of the largest corporations in the country – made donations totaling more than $1 million to the campaign war chests of key senators. "It's a rare thing for members of Congress to go against the money these days," said Mansur Gidfar, spokesman for the anti-corruption group Represent.Us. "They know exactly which special interests they need to keep happy if they want to fund their re-election campaigns or secure a future job as a lobbyist."[35]

All combined, the hypermobility of transnational corporations, the creation of money by deregulated banks, and the cozy relationship between government and big business have resulted in a profoundly undemocratic global order with deepening impacts on people and the planet.

This enormous and obfuscated system can feel so vast and all encompassing that we tend to forget that the world hasn't always been this way. Although we of course can't go back, the stories of land-based indigenous cultures can show us the vital importance of local knowledge and skills for utilizing local resources, to rebuild a genuinely sustainable relationship with the earth and with one another.

10

RETHINKING THE PAST

In the logs of Christopher Columbus and in other reports of first encounters with indigenous societies, native peoples are commonly described as "healthy", "kind", "generous" and "happy".[1] Today, however, anyone portraying traditional cultures in such a positive light is likely to be accused of "romanticizing the past." Pre-modern life is now generally described in terms of deprivation, hardship, insecure subsistence, constant drudgery and early death. But this depiction of the past is even more misleading than supposedly idealized portrayals.

In describing the past, the dominant narrative tends to start with the horrors of Dickensian London. There is almost no mention of life before the Enclosures and the Industrial Revolution, which tore apart the social fabric that supported land-based ways of life. Life in London by that time was indeed brutal, with horrific exploitation of people and nature. This is what we tend to think of when we say that life today is a vast improvement over 'the past'.

But a few pockets of indigenous land-based ways of life have persisted into the modern era, and those provide a more accurate window on the features of a localized culture and economy. As described earlier, I had the privilege of getting to know one such culture – Ladakh – when it was still largely unaffected by the global economy, and when its traditional values and structures were still intact. This experience provided me with an almost unique perspective on place-based cultures that I believe is profoundly relevant to the search for healthier and more sustainable ways of life.

Protected by high mountain passes, Ladakh had been spared the impacts of colonialism and, until recently, development. When I arrived in 1975, Ladakh's traditional community-based culture and economy still functioned well.

It did not take me long to realize that in this harsh and barren high-altitude environment, the Ladakhis were actually *prospering*. They had little money, but there was no hunger, no poverty, no unemployment, and no homelessness – most people, in fact, lived in spacious homes on their own land. Children and the elderly were valued contributors to society, and women had remarkably high status. Despite having only animal power and simple tools – and a very short growing season in which to produce all their own food – the Ladakhis still enjoyed more leisure time than most people in the West.

Most importantly, the Ladakhis exhibited an incredible, active *joie de vivre*. After living with them for many years I realized that they simply didn't suffer from our neuroses – they were truly at ease and happy.

But as I have described, Ladakh was dramatically changed by the global economy in less than a generation. Development effectively dismantled the local economy: subsidized, chemically-produced food from the Indian plains flooded the market, making the local organic agriculture that had sustained people for hundreds of years suddenly seem uneconomical.

Development had negative impacts on the environment as well: once-pristine streams became polluted with plastic bags and flashlight batteries, and the thin air became fouled by diesel fumes from growing numbers of trucks and generators. The status of women suffered, as development shifted decision-making power away from the household and village – where women were highly respected – to male-dominated bureaucracies in distant urban centers. Advertising and media, meanwhile, implicitly informed the Ladakhis that urban life is glamorous, exciting and easy, and that the life of a farmer is backward and dull.

Because of these changes, there was a loss of self-esteem, an increase in pettiness and small-minded gossip, and unprecedented levels of divisiveness and friction. As described in Chapter 4, the intense competition for jobs and political power in the modern economy even led to violent conflict between Buddhists and Muslims, groups that had lived peacefully side by side in Ladakh for centuries.

Again, the sudden changes in Ladakh were only apparent to me because I had arrived early enough to see the old culture when it was intact. Anyone visiting Ladakh for the first time today would have no way of knowing just how well the old place-based culture worked.

If we look closely we can see that the same transformation I observed in Ladakh has unfolded in cultures and communities around the world. In my native Sweden the process of modernization dismantled smaller-scale, diversified food production in favor of large-scale agriculture, and weakened rural community life in favor of rapid urbanization. As people found themselves alone in high-rise apartments – dependent on technology and distant bureaucracies rather than on each other – feminine values and the ties between family, community, and the land were all weakened. By the 1980s more than half of the dwellings in Stockholm were inhabited by one person living alone.[2] At the same time, not surprisingly, loneliness, alcoholism and suicide were on the rise.[3]

Even in Spain, where my husband and I lived during the 1980s, change was evident from one year to the next: farmers' markets replaced by supermarkets stocked with imported foods; walkable, rural towns abandoned for big traffic-congested cities; plastic packaging choking the countryside; people too stressed out and busy working to stop for the traditional *siesta* or for a drink with friends.

It can be difficult for those who live at the far end of these trends – who have grown up in a modern, urbanized, English-speaking society – to comprehend what is being lost. This is especially true because most of their experience of smaller towns and rural communities is limited to places that were sapped of vitality long ago – places the young abandoned for the big cities, places where people felt marginalized and where small-mindedness, gossip and prejudice thrived.

If you haven't experienced villages, towns or rural areas where the inhabitants have genuine control over their own lives, it's understandable that you might find the idea of 'one world' appealing – a high-tech paradise where everyone looks familiar, speaks English, and shares similar 'progressive' worldviews and cultural habits.

But it would be a mistake to generalize from what we find in many down-at-the-heels small communities, which have been robbed of their self-esteem, self-reliance and resources, in many cases over hundreds of years.

The vitally important need to adapt to diversity has been buried and hidden during 500 years of conquest, colonialism, and economic development – a long process of globalization that has imposed monocultural ideas and practices around the world. Even in the search for sustainability there has been a tendency to assume that 'one size fits all' – that people everywhere should live in 'smart cities', drive hybrid cars, and embrace vegetarianism. Place-based, localized solutions have no place in this monocultural version of progress.

But there is, of course, no one single formula for life: the need for diversity extends down to every blade of grass, to every earthworm and songbird, and to the identities of unique individuals within a myriad of different cultures. Erasing diversity is simply incompatible with life. For that reason, globalization – which systematically replaces diversity with monoculture – is also incompatible with life.

This does not mean we should idealize life in the past. In Ladakh, for example, infant mortality rates were higher in the traditional culture, and people were less comfortable than modern people in the West, especially in the winter. But if we look at what's most important, the old culture really worked: it proved itself sustainable over many hundreds of years, and people were really happy.

Localization isn't about returning to the past. Instead it asks us to recognize what older cultures often did well: they relied on local resources and local knowledge to meet people's material needs, and as a result did so with a minimum of environmental impact; they put a high value on community ties, which enabled them to meet people's psychological need for connection and security. These are important lessons to keep in mind as we search for solutions to our current crises.

Counter-development

Local Futures has worked in Ladakh for four decades to counter the overly idealistic impressions of modern urban life that are so destructive to the traditional culture. We have run Reality Tours to the West for Ladakhi leaders in order to reveal the darker sides of life in the industrialized world – from homelessness and drug addiction to the warehousing of the elderly – that people in the so-called 'developing' world are usually unaware of. These tours include engagement with people and projects working in the West to rebuild community and to find a more ecological path – a path that mimics many aspects of traditional Ladakhi life: organic agriculture, natural fibers and building materials, and experiential learning. In Ladakh we have worked with local community leaders to introduce small-scale renewable energy technologies that can improve material standards of living, without tying the Ladakhis into the global fossil fuel economy.

A long time ago I coined the term 'counter-development' to describe our work in Ladakh. It's good to see that other organizations are now doing similar work. Among them is Africa Organics, an indigenous organization that works in rural Gambia. The group works with remote villagers, letting them know that they have a lot of things most people in the Western world lack: land of their own, clean water, fertile soil, and knowledge of how to grow food and build houses in a sustainable fashion. In this way, they lend prestige to Gambia's traditional knowledge and skills. Their Home Farm Project works with young people who want to stay in (or return to) their villages, helping them establish diverse, sustainable farms.

There is a great need for activities that deconstruct the myths in the dominant narrative and inform people about the realities on the ground in both North and South. I now call this type of work 'big picture activism'.

11

BIG PICTURE
ACTIVISM

The forces pushing further globalization can easily seem too powerful to stop. But because more and more of us are becoming aware of its disastrous consequences for people and the planet, I truly believe that the chances for meaningful change are greater today than ever before. As I continue to speak to people around the world about the need for a shift from global to local, I have noticed an increasing openness to these ideas, and a recognition that the dominant narrative is hollow. People are aware that something is fundamentally wrong, and that minor tinkering with the current system is not the solution. What's needed now is a critical mass with a clear understanding of the root cause of the crises we face, and solutions that are meaningful. Helping to create that critical mass is the goal of what I call 'big picture activism'.

We need information campaigns that spell out the basics of *how* globalization is being pushed, and what its real-world consequences are. Greater 'eco-literacy' – i.e. both economic and ecological literacy – is also needed, in order to make clear how localization is the key to both human prosperity and a healthy planet.

This kind of awareness-raising is a vital form of action, and is a necessary stage in the building of successful movements. Before organic food was available on the market, for example, proponents of organic agriculture had to invest many years in education campaigns to inform people of what 'organic' meant, and about the costs of chemical agriculture to both health and the environment.

But many people want to move straight to action. They say, "We already know that the economy's the problem and that corporations have too much power – we don't need to keep discussing that." It is true that most of us have a sense that economic forces are behind environmental and social justice problems, but few understand how the global economic system undermines individual and cultural self-esteem; how it exacerbates ethnic, racial, and religious conflict; and how it damages our physical and psychological health. Nor is the majority aware that trade treaties have given corporations and banks so much power that they have become a de-facto global government – ruling behind the scenes regardless of whether a 'left' or 'right' party has been elected. A broad, global-to-local perspective can strengthen the effectiveness of those who already oppose corporate rule, while helping to cut across traditional left-right barriers to illuminate our much broader commonalities.

Once people wake up to the fact that the same economic policies are the underlying driver of everything from job insecurity and poverty to climate chaos and the rise of extremism, we can transcend isolated single-issue campaigns and build movements that are big and resilient enough to recapture democratic power from global monopolies. It's also my conviction that once people in the industrialized West wake up to the systemic roots of their spiritual, emotional and psychological sufferings, massive energy will be mobilized for fundamental change.

Connecting the dots in this way is a critical aspect of building support for a fundamental shift in direction. And what we have to offer is much more than just a theoretical framework: we can point to powerful, fast-growing movements for economic change – the New Economy Coalition, the Post-Growth Alliance, the New Economy and Social Innovation Forum, the Wellbeing Economy Alliance, Systemic Alternatives, and many others. Rather than pinning their hopes on telegenic representatives of the left or right that offer essentially the same recipe for 'progress' (equal parts economic growth, trade-promotion, high technology and corporate sponsorship), these movements seek fundamental structural change.

Perhaps even more importantly, we can make visible the rapid worldwide proliferation of localization initiatives and their real-world impacts. In this way, we can weave a new narrative that lets people know that a different future is already in the making. We can show that in North and South, in the city and the country, people are rebuilding connections to others and to Nature, with immediate spiritual, psychological, and practical benefits.

What's more, increasing numbers of people around the world are waking up to the central role of trade treaties in enabling corporate rule, and these treaties have become key targets for activists seeking to halt the global juggernaut. Since the historic protests against the WTO in Seattle in 1999, there have been demonstrations at nearly every major international trade meeting, from the G8 to the World Economic Forum. Protesters have sometimes numbered in the hundreds of thousands, bringing worldwide attention to a process that had previously been hidden from public view. Just six years before the Seattle demonstrations, NAFTA was pushed through with relatively little resistance. As corporate negotiators tried to exert the same control over government policy with the TPP and the TTIP, they met with heavy resistance – not just from concerned citizens, but even from many elected representatives.

Rethinking assumptions

Today's consumer culture is based on myths and misinformation that paralyze and confuse people with contradictory ideas. A segment on the evening news asks whether consumer spending is adequate to keep the economy going; a few minutes later it tells us that consumer greed is destroying the world.

Stories that place the individual consumer at the center of our global problems are rife. Recently, there has been much discussion about the 'psychology of denial', which argues that climate change is worsening because human beings are not facing up to the seriousness of the crisis, and are clinging stubbornly to their wasteful habits. Absent from this discussion is the fact that, at every level, subsidies, taxes and regulations are being used to support and promote energy-intensive and wasteful production, insane international trade and the ubiquitous promotion of consumerism – against all of which individual consumer habits pale in significance.

None of us voted to put this system in place. Instead, it grew out of blind faith in outdated colonial assumptions, and it is primarily our collective ignorance of the workings of this system that allows it to continue, unabated. When we hear talk of economic growth, therefore, we need to be literate about the assumptions underlying job creation statistics (see "Loss of livelihoods", Chapter 3), and be willing to start a discussion about "growth for *whom*, and at the expense of *what*?"

We also need to encourage a deeper, broader look at what we call 'progress'. The linear, econometric view of progress – the version that Bill Gates, Steven Pinker & Co. would have us believe – portrays the past as something we are fortunate to have escaped from, and tells us that economic growth and technological advance makes ours the most privileged generation ever to walk the Earth. We need to temper that view with a meaningful discussion of what we have lost: the majority have been fragmented into nuclear families, cut off from the supports of community, denied meaningful productive activity, deprived of access to land and to healthy food and excluded from genuine decision-making power. We've been robbed of time – an essential ingredient for meaningful relationships, love, care and empathy. Almost all of our activities have been commercialized – and while this makes the 'growth' charts look healthy, a deeper examination reveals that it has led to severe emotional and social impoverishment.

When taking a critical, historical view of progress, it's equally important to distinguish cultural progress from economic growth. It is true that, over the past hundred years or so, shifts in values have occurred within the Western world that can generally be termed 'progressive': we have moved away from cultural supremacy, developing respect for other beliefs, races and cultures. And we have dramatically shifted away from patriarchy, towards a clear and conscious embrace of women, the feminine and gender fluidity.

The economic trajectory, however, has remained out of touch with those changing values, and has continued on a straight line from colonialism. From the very beginning, the colonial project has been about undermining local economies and extracting value from them for a centralized elite; unfortunately, as this book has shown, the cultural shift in values has not yet succeeded in transforming our economic system. Wealth inequality has expanded to record extremes, and slavery, cultural destruction and domination over nature have only become more insidious. Meanwhile, behind the egalitarian façade of the capitalist system, the growth of corporate power is impoverishing millions, leaving them deeply insecure and therefore vulnerable to xenophobic and racist rhetoric. Awareness of the 'big picture' is necessary to realign an outdated economic system with our genuinely progressive social and cultural values.

I also hear people say, "the system is going to collapse of its own accord, so there's no need to waste time trying to change it." But despite its deep flaws and contradictions, the economic system may outlive much of the natural and social world. Many years ago, the Swiss economist H.C. Binswanger convinced me that deregulated capital – money de-linked from any standard or limit – could keep multiplying endlessly, even as ecosystems and societies crash. In other words, the economy could keep growing until the last tree falls. A depressing scenario, and one that we must do everything we can to prevent.

Unfortunately, many have completely given up on the idea of fundamentally changing the system. People think it's too hard – that shifting social institutions is beyond the ability of even the most powerful movement. But it's vital to keep in mind that the road we're currently on is supported by *our* laws and funded by *our* taxes. Unless we let our voices be heard in active support of another direction, we are acquiescing to the continued hijacking of our social institutions in the interest of further centralization and profit extraction.

As big and overwhelming as the global system seems, shifting direction would actually be easier, in practical terms, than continuing to globalize. In order for globalization to continue, local councils, hospitals and schools would have to be further amalgamated; businesses would have to merge with ever larger ones to survive; cities that are already bursting at the seams would have to grow still larger; and the massive infrastructure for global trade would have to be expanded still further. The global economy would have to be continually re-engineered to facilitate ever more centralized control, taking more power from democratic institutions. It would require immense investments of money and natural resources, all the while ripping apart the fabric of ecosystems, societies and cultures, and leaving more and more people jobless and insecure.

In order to localize, the key step is simply to redirect existing systemic supports – away from the global and towards the local. This would immediately begin to lessen our resource use, to regenerate the social fabric and expand the possibilities for far less destructive, job-rich, local employment.

Nonetheless, even committed activists sometimes say, "there's no point in trying – governments won't listen no matter what we do." It is true that millions of people marched against the Iraq war, and yet policymakers took us into that senseless and destructive conflict. It is true that millions are opposed to gas fracking and nuclear energy, and yet governments continue to promote those technologies. But the potential for people to really be heard will grow exponentially when they move beyond a fragmented perspective to focus on the common thread that runs through all their concerns. A 'new economy' movement – one that is clear about what we are for, not just what we are against – has far greater potential to succeed than almost any single-issue campaign.

An emphasis on inner transformation can be another stumbling block. The New Age movement has done tremendous good in encouraging millions of people to listen to their hearts and to the wisdom of ancient indigenous cultures. This deeper consciousness creates a yearning to turn away from the competition and consumerism of the global economy and to build more loving relationships with others and the Earth. This emphasis led many people to focus almost exclusively on the 'inner' dimension, on 'thinking positively', and personal change. And many among them tended to look down on activists who seemed fixated on the 'outer' world of social and environmental activism.

In the activist community, meanwhile, many have ignored their personal, inner needs, while emphasizing 'outer' practical and political change. Even though their work is usually born of altruism, ignoring the inner dimension has often hampered their efforts. Neglecting peace of mind and inner reflection and focusing on the negative can lead to self-righteousness and helpless anger, and eventually to burnout, conflict, and alienation. Big picture activism makes clear that our problems have both an inner and an outer dimension, and that solving them requires working on both levels.

Big picture activism does not point a finger at individual politicians, CEOs or bankers. As I argued at the outset, our destructive economic system continues to expand primarily because of ignorance. The economic pundits that promote this growth model have been trained to look at flows of money and numerical representations of the world, and are shielded from many of the real-life social and ecological consequences of their abstract models. The CEOs of large corporations and banks are driven by speculative markets to meet short-term profit and growth targets, and so have even less ability to contemplate the overall impact of their actions. Even concerned citizens, including activists, can find it difficult to see the many hidden ways that both their consumer choices and taxes end up supporting an energy-intensive, job- and soul-destroying economy.

This awareness takes us beyond a politics of identity, beyond blaming individual people, and – crucially – beyond self-blame. We can focus instead on changing the 'I' to a 'we' – coming together at the community level as well as the political level.

The way forward lies not in anger and confrontation, but in actively encouraging peaceful, broad-based, systemic change.

Awareness can spread like fire, and it's empowering to realize that we don't necessarily need to convince our political and economic leaders – who tend to be too locked into their misguided assumptions – or that sector of the population that is deeply immersed in consumerism. Despite enormous financial and time pressures, there are large numbers of engaged and concerned people who are working to make the world a better place. They may be focused on improving their children's school, working to end cruelty to animals, to protect wildlife, to reduce waste and CO_2 emissions, to feed the hungry, or to promote spiritual and ethical values. No matter what problem they're addressing, the economy is a common thread that links them all.

In recent years, many individuals and organizations involved in these separate campaigns have begun to embrace a holistic approach that moves beyond single issues. As a result, a broad, big-picture analysis is beginning to build a diverse, united movement – a movement with the potential to become the largest that the world has ever seen.

12

THE ECONOMICS
OF HAPPINESS

Let me introduce you to two dear friends of mine, Tim and Caroline. They are young, sensitive people, who are painfully aware of the brokenness of the world they live in. They have grown up seeing news images of bombs killing innocent people; they have lost friends to suicide. They have struggled with feelings of worthlessness and depression; they have seen people stricken by chronic illnesses and ecosystems damaged beyond repair.

But they have fallen in love with each other, and have had two beautiful children, Xan and Ella. Bringing children into the world while remaining alert to the intensifying sufferings of that world is an act of bravery. They know the path Xan and Ella have been set on is fraught with dangers: school will encourage competition and hyper-individualism, the media will tell them they're not beautiful or talented enough, and when they grow up, who knows if there will be meaningful jobs for them to occupy – or worse, a healthy planet for them to live on?

Tim and Caroline have made a promise to themselves: they will do whatever they can to provide Xan and Ella the support they need to flourish, to give them the future they deserve. They will do everything in their power to build strong and lasting community with others, to seek out a healthy educational environment for them, to protect them from advertising and from the harmful influence of screens, to nourish their bodies with wholesome food, to encourage deep enchantment with the natural world.

Of course, there are places around the world where couples like Tim and Caroline can go to build a better life with like-minded folk. But even these communities face the numerous challenges of straddling two worlds moving in different directions: they encounter money issues, regulatory restrictions, community members picked up and moved around for work. They grapple with the contradictions of developing place-based cultures in a fragmenting, globalizing world.

Until we work together to bring about an economic shift from global to local, people like Tim and Caroline will be going against the current to keep their loved ones safe from the wounds inflicted by an inhuman system. And they will not always succeed; they will regularly have to choose between making money and spending time with their kids, between living outside the pervasive influence of the consumer culture and interacting with the wider world, between focusing on their own immediate needs and trying to make the world a better place. They risk internalizing blame for their mistakes, burning out and breaking down.

And yet, in this system, Tim and Caroline are the lucky ones. They at least have access to information about what food is healthy for their bodies, what poisons to avoid, and enough money to enable them to make choices. They can pay the mortgage on a comfortable home with a garden big enough to grow some vegetables and to let Xan and Ella play outdoors. They have parents who live in the same country and are sometimes around to help raise the kids. And Tim and Caroline have each other. Sadly, their situation is a distant dream for an increasing proportion of the global population, many of whom are single parents, or working multiple jobs just to pay the rent, or living in slums, or in conflict zones, or all of the above. Many of these people have little choice but to completely shut out awareness of a broken system, because they simply have no foreseeable way out of it.

If we hope to change the harsh realities people all around the world are facing, we need more than just the courage to battle uphill – we need to work together to create an *economics of happiness*. With a big-picture, strategic restructuring of economic supports, we can make healthy local food the cheapest and most accessible food on the market, and local, community-based, stable livelihoods the most abundant jobs available. We can create the structural basis for community, which offers deep psychological benefits and puts care for our children and care for the land back at the center of our daily activities. We can take back control of our own lives and create the conditions that are a prerequisite for joy, peace and sustainability.

Today's fast-paced global economy demands mobility, competitiveness, and individualism, and induces a fear of being vulnerable and dependent; of growing old. Localization, by contrast, answers our deep longing for love and connection – the cornerstones of well-being and contentment.

There is ever more research into the deep healing that springs from reconnection to nature and to community, and from spiritually awakening to the oneness of life. Tried and tested therapies for recovering addicts, like Alcoholics Anonymous and Narcotics Anonymous, which focus on mutual support and contact with higher spiritual purpose, have been demonstrating compelling results for quite some time. Recently, a myriad of other methods has emerged, including a proliferation of wilderness-immersion and animal-connection therapies. Localization provides the economic structures that regenerate the fabric of interdependence, promoting daily contact with others and with the plants and animals in the natural world around us. In this way, what are now expensive weekend therapies for a minority could become a fundamental way of life for people all over the world.

Through renewing community structures, we stand to regain so much of what we have lost. Even within thoroughly industrialized and colonized parts of the world – from British cities to South African slums – it wasn't that long ago that friends and family were generally not so far apart and children could run free, with neighbors and relatives to keep an eye out for them. This reduced the workload on mothers, allowing them to more fully participate in everyday life.

In Ladakh, as in many indigenous cultures, economic structures that promoted collaboration between people and other beings were reinforced by spiritual teachings that reminded people every day that their own well-being and the well-being of others were one and the same. Modernity has brought a stark reversal of these teachings; a highly competitive economy tells us that my well-being is at the *expense* of yours. We are bombarded 24/7 with imagery (the 'teachings' of the consumer religion) compelling us to consume more, to get ahead, to become a 'somebody' instead of a 'nobody'.

When the global economy moved into Ladakh, I began to see a rapid shift towards the patterns of consumerism and psychological insecurity we are familiar with in the West. In the modern world, relationships have become distant and monetized, intergenerational contact has been replaced by flattened peer groups, and the social fabric has frayed. Lonely and cut off, we can fall prey to the idea that, to get the love and appreciation we need, we have to become 'famous'. Even three-year-old Ella can be heard saying that she wants to become a famous singer when she grows up.

The notion of 'fame' in the global media stands in direct contrast to the kind of validation individuals receive in more localized societies. In traditional Ladakh – and even in the villages of England and Spain where I have lived – I have seen how a web of enduring relationships fulfilled the natural and very legitimate human desire to be seen, to be heard, to be appreciated and loved. In a human-scale context, everyone is (as it were) 'famous'; instead of comparing themselves to distant stars, their role-models are real-life people, none of whom are totally perfect. People are recognized for both their strengths and weaknesses; in Ladakh it was known that Dolma was a beautiful singer but not so good at dancing, while Stanzin was a better dancer but was not as good at singing. Nevertheless, Dolma and Stanzin would regularly join in with the singing and dancing at community events. Children in Ladakh grew up learning how to sing, dance and make music *together*. It was never a question of being perfect. By contrast, in the hyper-competitive, commercial culture of the West, children are pressured from an early age to specialize and to be 'the best' in their field. In this way we have created a culture of division, with a few stars and vast numbers of spectators.

By localizing we move away from a fame-obsessed culture of insecurity and competition to create participatory cultures instead. Strong communities and stable livelihoods offer people the chance to put down roots and develop secure, place-based identities wherever they are. In localized economies, individuals and families are not regularly scattered by blind economic forces; they instead rely on more stable economic opportunities that allow them to work closer to home, utilizing skills and systems adapted to place.

Local economies are not some kind of prison, preventing people from moving elsewhere or choosing to travel to other cultures to experience other ways of life. On the contrary, localization moves us away from the homogenizing influence of the global consumer monoculture towards enriched cultural diversity. In this way, our opportunities for authentic encounters and exchange with other cultures are far greater.

Shifting from global to local is a systemic strategy to move us from a fragmented and confused world dominated by almost-invisible, distant economic forces, towards an interconnected and diversified world that is the foundation of happy individuals, peaceful societies and a healthy planet.

Wherever we are, we can start the journey. We can seek out like-minded individuals with the goal of encouraging deeper connections. In order to relate open-heartedly and foster such connections, we must have the courage to reject the posturing of the consumer culture, and to expose our needs and vulnerabilities. We can move away from the fear and self-consciousness that keep us apart, and create more participatory cultures of sharing and caring. By reconnecting with the sources of our food, perhaps even growing some of our own, we can nurture a deep, empathetic connection to nature and learn to appreciate the cycles of the seasons and the characteristics of flora and fauna. Quieting the chattering mind – through prayer, meditation, song, dance or yoga – can help free us of the pressures imposed by the global economy and can deeply rejuvenate and inspire us. In these ways, we can begin to make choices that are good for us as individuals as well as for our community and for society as a whole.

Throughout human history, our cultural traditions, our societies, our personalities, even our bodies have evolved in connection with community and nature. The globalizing economy has severed these connections with false promises: that technology will solve all of our problems, that economic growth is the key to progress, that more stuff and more money will make us happy.

The word is getting out, however, that our global economic system is simply not working. Around the world we are witnessing a truly positive cultural evolution. We are re-learning what ancient indigenous cultures knew: that the 'inner' and the 'outer', and the human and the non-human, are inextricably intertwined. We are beginning to see the world within us – to experience more consciously the great interdependent web of life, of which we ourselves are part.

CODA

A CONVERSATION WITH WENDELL BERRY

Wendell Berry is a much-loved American farmer, poet, essayist, and outspoken advocate for land-based ways of life. For me, he has also been a valued friend, colleague and inspiration for over 30 years. I had a chance to speak with him recently about issues of concern to both of us – as well as to readers of this book.

HELENA: Your words of wisdom are especially valuable today, when so many people are feeling desperate and depressed. Many are giving up on humankind. They say things like "human beings are just ignorant, stupid and greedy, and we deserve to extinguish ourselves."

WENDELL: That seems to me to be a cheap way out. I think that there's some merit to be found among us, and some merit to be found in our history. There's a lot of bad in it, no question about that, but the interesting thing is to try to solve the problem, not escape it.

HELENA: It's also important to realize that the real problem is not human nature, but what I think of as an inhuman *system*. One of the biggest problems we're facing is that the system has become so big that we can't see what we're doing and what we're contributing to – our economic system is of such an inhuman scale that it has become like a giant machine – a global juggernaut that's pushing us all into fear and a terrible sense of scarcity. I guess that's why we both believe in a scale whereby humans are at least able to see the mess they create.

WENDELL: What one has to say to begin with is that as humans we are limited in intelligence, and we have really no very reliable foresight. So none of us will come up with answers to the whole great problem. What we can do is judge our behavior, our history, and our present situation by a better standard than 'efficiency' or 'profit' or those measures that we're still using to determine economic decisions. The standard that I always come back to is the health of the world, which is the same as our own personal health. We can't distinguish our health from the health of everything else. And we know enough from the ecologists now to know that health is a very complex and un-understandable complexity of relationships that makes the world whole. And insofar as it's whole, it's not only able to survive, it's also beautiful. And to subtract arbitrarily for merely economic reasons any part of that whole is a great fault. So by the standard of health we have to be inclusive in our charity toward everything else. This is a kind of neighborliness, and we have fairly good instructions about how to treat our neighbors. Our neighbors are not just our friends. They are our enemies, and the nonhuman creatures with whom we share the world.

HELENA: Rather than those economic measures you referred to, the goal needs to be human and ecological well-being. And when people are more dependent on the living community around them – both the human and the nonhuman – then it becomes obvious that their well-being is connected to the well-being of the other. It's in this long-distance system dependent on abstract ideas and abstract institutions where we don't even see our masters – the big global banks and other institutions – that we move into a type of ignorance and even madness.

WENDELL: It seems to me that it all depends upon our ability to accept limits. And the present economic system doesn't even acknowledge limits. But if we acknowledge the existence of limits and the necessity of honoring them, it's possible to imagine an economy that takes care of the good things that we have in our immediate neighborhood, rather than an economy that 'develops resources' – which is to say turning resources into riches (which is to say money) – which leads almost inevitably to destruction. Money is an abstraction. Goods are particular, and always available within limits – natural limits, and the rightful limits of our consumption.

HELENA: And in order for us to see those limits, we need a more human-scale, localized economy.

WENDELL: It would mean even more if we said a community economy, and we meant by economy the original sense of 'household management' or 'housekeeping'. That would imply taking the best possible care of the life supports of, first, the household economy, then the neighborhood economy, then the community economy. And we can go on from there on the principle of community, if we take it in the sense of 'what we all have in common', and an obligation to take care of all of it. But it will only be manageable locally, and within limits. The limits, among other things, of our own intelligence and our own capacity to act responsibly.

HELENA: What I've seen in ancient traditional cultures is that even the language reminded people that their experiential knowledge was really the only reliable knowledge. So for instance in ancient Tibetan you couldn't say "in my garden right now the apples are ripe" and then next sentence say, "In China such-and-such is happening." Instead you would be forced to show that you had never been to China and that you had heard second- or third-hand what is happening there. One of the great tragedies has been this shift towards trusting second-hand knowledge more than we trust experiential knowledge, and in fact *denigrating* experiential knowledge as anecdotal and worthless. And of course this has been reinforced by numerical, and very reductionist modern science.

WENDELL: I think what you're applying there is simply the fundamental rule of all the human disciplines. And that rule is that you have to know what you're talking about. You have to come with evidence. And this applies across the board, from the court of law to the laboratory of the scientist. If you make an assertion, you have to back it up with something you actually know and can demonstrate. So we have to distinguish between knowledge and speculation, knowledge and wishful thinking, knowledge and projections or predictions. All that is simply a part of responsible thought.

HELENA: But of course now we have science and knowledge for profit, which can lead to very shoddy proof. In Chinese medicine, for example, things have been tested and tried for literally ten thousand years – but in the modern world the time between so-called discovery and market application is sometimes measured in months. Meanwhile, the impact of these new discoveries has the potential to affect all life on earth – for instance, genetic manipulation.

WENDELL: The issue there again, it seems to me, is the acceptance of a limit. Science that accepts limits would do no harm to an ecosystem or a human body. This is very different from the kind of science that is pursuing Truth with a capital T, and will do anything, any violence, to make that discovery. And too frequently it turns out to be product development. And the people who make the discovery are incapable of controlling its application. The nuclear scientists who developed the atomic bomb are a very good example. But so are chemists who develop toxic substances for a limited use that they have in mind, but then turn it loose on the market and into the world. So you develop a chemical to control weeds in crops and you ask only the question of whether or not the weeds are controlled; you don't ask what happens when it runs off into the rivers.

HELENA: This is why there has to be the precautionary principle, as Rachel Carson reminded us. But the only entities really capable of enforcing the precautionary principle are governments – and the trade treaties and the globalizing economy have given giant multinational companies more and more power over governments. We've seen these last thirty years the enormous damage that this power shift created. And then with the financial breakdown in 2008, it was so clear that we needed regulation, but it didn't happen.

WENDELL: The global economy is almost by definition not subject to regulation. And this simply means that corporations can pursue economic advantage without limit, wherever in the world those advantages are to be found. And as I've thought of it in the last several years, it has seemed to me that we've had a global economy about 500 years – ever since the time of Columbus. And this allowed us to think that if we don't have some necessity of life here we can get it from somewhere else. This is the most damaging idea that we've ever had. It's still with us, still current, and it still excuses local plunder and theft and enslavement. It's an extreme fantasy or unreality, the idea that if we don't have it here we can get it somewhere else – if we use it up here we can get it somewhere else. It's the stuff of fantasy. Finally, it's wrong, it's simply a falsehood.

HELENA: What's very frightening is that from the centers of power in the corporate world there's a recognition that globalization is not working, and that a shift from global to local is needed – but what they're talking about is the opposite of what you and I talk about. It's about giant multinationals using robots to make washing machines in America instead of producing them in China.

WENDELL: This makes all the world a colony.

HELENA: Yes.

WENDELL: I'm a rural American, and moreover a Kentuckian. I live in a state that has been a colony all my life, and probably ever since the Civil War, at least. We're a coal-producing state. Some of our counties are the richest in the world in their natural endowment, and the result of that is that they now have land that is virtually destroyed and some of the poorest people. This is the result of a limitless economy. And the only recourse that we have is to try to understand what we have here that's worth our keeping, and then to discover ways to keep it – and that is to say that we have to have recourse to this movement towards local economies. We should fulfill our needs and export the surplus. We should never export the necessities of our own lives. I think the test, the ultimate test, is whether or not we live in beautiful places. Wherever ugliness has crept in, we have the first symptom of exploitation and exhaustion.

HELENA: And illness. You know, it's so interesting how beauty and health go together. And the ugliness is part of the sickness, of land and of people.

WENDELL: If we have a loved one who's in ill health, we say, "you don't look good". And by that we mean that some kind of ugliness has crept into your body.

HELENA: It isn't just beauty alone: when we talk about health we're also talking about happiness – we're talking about inner psychological and spiritual well-being, and about care and nurturing of others and of yourself. So again it's all connected. You also mentioned what might be called a 'movement' towards local economies. Are you a bit resistant to using that notion, of a movement?

WENDELL: The word 'movement'? (Laugh). Yes, I wrote an essay once called "In Distrust of Movements". My quarrel with movements, and the reason I use it in quotation marks, so to speak, is that they tend to be specialized. For example there's a movement now about climate change, and it has become extremely specialized, while the actual solution to a problem like that is to have an economy that takes care of everything – an inclusive economy, not just an economy of moneymaking. And so I'm always a little anxious about movements. They turn into fads in a way, and then they peter out because they're too specialized.

HELENA: Exactly. And it's so frightening that the climate movement has become specialized to the point of being destructive, particularly when you have talk of market-based 'solutions' like carbon trading and carbon offsets. So my plea is for what I call 'big picture activism', to support a shift from global to local. When we see the multiple benefits of localizing, it becomes clear that it's not about specialization, it's about adaptation to diversity. I often say that localism is 'the -ism that could end all -isms', because it has to entail this adaptation to diversity. This is the opposite of a movement that wants to impose a standard solution or a standard anything. Any kind of monoculture is deadly.

WENDELL: That's right. Localism would cease to be an -ism just as soon as the local people went to work locally. One of the things that's wrong with these great movements is that they're not telling people to go home and go to work in good ways to improve things. They're movements to bring pressure on political leaders. And to that extent it's something of a distraction from the real problems, which are all local.

HELENA: Here is a point where you and I might differ. Because I believe that we need both 'resistance' and 'renewal' simultaneously. What I mean by 'resistance' is first of all linking together locally to resist the advances of the top-down global monoculture in all its destructive forms. But it also means linking up with other groups around the country and even around the world to push for a kind of democracy where people have a choice. Do they want to be replaced by robots? Do they want to be enslaved to send off the food they need for their local economy? Or would they rather shift their regulations, taxes, and subsidies to support local economies worldwide? So in that sense I do believe that at the same time as we start the work at home we can also raise our voices to have a unified call to come back home.

WENDELL: You're really asking me, Helena, whether in addition to my insistence on the importance of the local context and local work, I believe in policy changes. And the answer is of course I do. And I have done a good bit of that work. Wes Jackson and his people at the Land Institute produced a farm policy called the '50-year farm bill', and what that proposes essentially is converting our agriculture from an 80% dependence on annual crops and a 20% dependence on perennials to the opposite – an 80% dependence on perennials and a 20% dependence on annuals. And that change, which would be a policy change, would cure a lot of problems, including to a considerable extent the problem of global warming. That's a policy, and it's general, to the extent that it would be a policy that would be in force nationally. However, if it was done rightly, It would have to be applied in different ways in different places. And that would call for a high degree of local knowledge and local intelligence.

HELENA: That is why we must have local knowledge to survive. And it's being killed off, of course, with the death of languages, which is concomitant with the death of species.

WENDELL: As knowledge accumulates in place over a long-lived lifetime and over the successive lifetimes in families and communities, local knowledge becomes almost instinctive, and it sort of becomes a matter of the application of affection as well as methods.

HELENA: Yes, and I've seen exactly that in traditional cultures, and I've been so struck by how – for uprooted, urbanized people who struggle to get back to community and the land – how every decision is such a difficult one and there isn't that inherited and almost instinctive knowledge. We don't realize just how much we've lost and how much more we can still lose if we don't really understand the gift of that inherited local knowledge. Part of that gift is that we can actually have more time to do the things we enjoy, to play, to celebrate, to sing and make music together – to actually enjoy life, and the beauty around us. This is really an invitation to a richer, more joyous life.

WENDELL: I think that's true. My publisher Counterpoint Press has just published a book called *Round of a Country Year*, by my friend David Kline, who's an Amish bishop in Holmes County, Ohio. And Holmes County is a very good exhibit because it's the largest Amish settlement in the country, where farm after farm is a small-scale Amish family farm. David's book – which is really a kind of journal of what he did day by day throughout the year – is remarkable for its happiness. Nobody is overworked because plenty of people are there. The scale is right. They've accepted certain limits and people are rarely in a hurry. It's one of the happiest books I've read in a long time. And I would recommend that as an exhibit of exactly what you're talking about.

HELENA: Thank God that there are still some communities that are able to have that ratio of people to the work, to the land, to the provision of our basic needs. I saw that so clearly in Ladakh: how incredibly easy it was, because there were plenty of people during the harvest, during the building of a house. Everything was done in a leisurely way and with so much time for celebration and festivity as part of the work.

WENDELL: It's partly because a lot of it is traditional. They are extraordinarily skillful, and those things ease the hardships. I think the Amish success is really attributable to their ability to embrace, in an economic sense, the idea that we should love our neighbors as ourselves. If you love your neighbors, you won't replace your neighbor with a machine, let alone a robot.

HELENA: Let's talk a bit more about that. Look at how we were promised that the computer was going to give us this amazing new information society where there was no need for industry, and we could all live in our lovely villages and just work a little bit on our computers. And let's look at what's happened now, and what is likely to happen with every new wave of technology.

WENDELL: I think that that's suicidal – it's the operation of the death wish among us – that we don't any longer want to live the lives of our bodies, our physical lives. The idea that you can't exert yourself so far as to crank up your automobile window is absurd. But it's also the antipathy to the use of the body for anything... except maybe sex. And I suppose it won't be long until we have a robot that can do that for us. And that will be a very radical setback. (Laugh).

HELENA: Already now robots are looking after old people, robots acting as surrogate children... I've seen the difference between children having contact with and looking after their younger siblings and living animals instead of dead stuffed animals or dolls.

WENDELL: If you love somebody, you need to have ways to enact your love. And that would be in caretaking for the children and the old people. The putting-on of hands. That's the only way we can do it. We can't enact our love by hiring a robot to do it. And the same goes for the world. If we let machinery, whether it's a robot or not, intervene to too great an extent between us and the farmland or the forestland that we're using, we begin to destroy it. We begin to destroy what economists would call the 'resource'. And finally this has a very practical economic effect. One effect of course is disease.

HELENA: I so wish that more people understood just how much cancer and heart disease and so on are on the increase. Many people don't realize that; they keep believing it's just because we live longer.

WENDELL: Wes Jackson recently sent me a sign that he'd taken from a motel in Colorado that said "if you are pregnant or nursing a child, don't drink this water". This has nothing to do with longevity, this has to do with poison in the drinking water. I recently made an effort to find out why the native black willows have disappeared from my river. And in the process I discovered that some scientists had discovered – and published in a refereed journal – that there's too much glyphosate (that's Roundup) in Midwestern rivers. And I called a couple of those scientists and I said "I see you've found out there's too much glyphosate in Midwestern rivers." "Oh yes," they said, "there's far too much." I said, "can you tell me what the effect of that is?" And the answer was that "a lot of people would like to know." This is because of the difficulty of attaching a cause to an effect, in the world in general but especially in a large volume of moving water. So we know that the toxic chemicals are there, but we're going to have a very hard time finding out what the effect is. There is as you were saying a while ago a precautionary principle. And the precautionary principle says: don't put poison in the water.

HELENA: Yes, and don't do anything when you have no idea what the effects are.

WENDELL: We don't know much about the future and that again cautions us to keep our work on a proper scale, and not to do too much too quickly. Wes and I have talked at considerable length about the difference between behavior based on the assumption of ignorance and behavior based on the assumption that we already know or will soon know everything we need to know.

HELENA: Exactly. A physicist friend of mine in Germany tells me that what's so frightening is that modern science is so enamored of its ability to predict, and of its modeling and so on, but they are only operating within the sphere of the man-made world. In terms of understanding life – how a seed matures, how our bodies actually function – the ignorance is still enormous. Now the next step is to move into a world of not just robots but 3D printing, driverless cars (which again of course are robots)... It's very frightening that people are so locked into the man-made world. And they would tell us, Wendell, that we are utopian, that we are not being realistic. For them the real world is this commercial man-made world.

WENDELL: It's a strange utopia that depends on people being absolutely passive. And this again, it seems to me, has to do with the death wish, which is also the same thing as addiction. Addiction is manifested by much more than dependence on a drug. Our children are dying from drug addiction here in rural America, in my little corner of it. But while the addiction to drugs is receiving some attention, young people are also addicted to computers – it is exactly an addiction, and nobody is concerned about that. Again that addiction removes the person physically from the life of the world. So it does seem to me to be deathly, suicidal, and absolutely ruinous.

HELENA: Did you know that there are also, in some places, clinics where they take screen-addicted youth? I don't know if they have them in America, but they have them in South Korea.

WENDELL: That's very profitable of course, and that means that this really helps economic growth. If you can make money by selling an addictive device and then make money by curing people of their addiction – that's a great business plan.

HELENA: Just like lots of cancer and chemotherapy are nicely adding to GDP.

WENDELL: Yes, that's right. (Laugh). It all depends on unhappiness, sickness, ill-health, and the rest of it. Ugliness.

HELENA: But isn't it remarkable that so few environmentalists are joining us to just laugh at the notion of GDP? Once it's understood that GDP increases with breakdown, it seems we all should be linking hands to demand a fundamental shift in the economy.

WENDELL: One of the roots of the problem is the focus of environmentalists. The conservation movement for 100 years has, at least in this country, focused on wilderness preservation – places of spectacular rocks and waterfalls – at the expense of what I would call the 'economic landscapes' of farming, forestry, and mining. The politicians have kept the environmental movement quiet by designating wilderness areas. And in the meantime they've let the corporations run completely out of control, and extraordinarily destructively, in the economic landscapes, without any acknowledgement at all that the natural world is out there just the same as it is in the parks.

HELENA: At the same time what I find so inspiring is that in the localization movement communities around the world are rebuilding truly healthy economies by diversifying. Those are like little diamonds in the landscape, aren't they, of beauty and joy.

WENDELL: Those are the examples we need to study and look to. And always that localization depends on a revival of the neighborhood principle. People can only do this if they help each other, and accounts come in my mail of how farmers for instance have scaled back, diversified, and increased the number of people who are employed on the land. This, it seems to me, is the incontrovertible answer to these people who say "we need to give up on human nature, and as a favor to Nature, commit suicide."

HELENA: Another important point is that small, diversified farms always produce more per unit of land, water and energy than large monocultures. So we have to turn this lie around that there are too many people now to localize, too many people to have small farms. It's exactly the opposite.

WENDELL: Small farms make economic sense. They also produce more happiness, more beauty, more health – those things that aren't so quantifiable.

HELENA: ... and more thriving opportunities for wildness within the farm.

WENDELL: Yes. That's counter-intuitive, but the more boundaries you have in the farming landscapes, the more the land is divided by fence-rows, the more bushes you have. These shrubby fence-rows act as wildlife corridors and habitats.

HELENA: To change subjects a bit, what you do say when people ask you as an American what you think about Trump and the people who voted for Trump?

WENDELL: Well, there's far too much generalization now about rural America. The conservatives and the corporations have had their eye on rural America all along. And they've been turning it into money as fast as they can, which is to say destroying the land and the people. The liberals and the Democrats have discovered rural America now – a place about as foreign to them as it was to Columbus. They don't know anything about it and they've been condemning it out of hand as if everybody out here in rural America is a racist, sexist, backward, ignorant person. And this isn't true. The problem is that rural America has been a colony, certainly throughout my lifetime. I don't think anybody's paid attention to rural America since about 1945 or '50. Certainly not since 1952, when Eisenhower's Secretary of Agriculture said to the farmers: "get big or get out." They've just abandoned rural America to the corporations and the technologies. And now, if they would only look out here and try to learn what's here and the really terrible predicament we're in, they might be able to construct a policy platform that would be meaningful and would give people a real choice. People voted for Trump not because they liked him but because they saw no hope. They didn't feel that they could count on the other side. A minister friend of mine wrote me to say that the Trump voters' grandfathers were priced out of farming. Their parents experienced a generation of union-supported good wages. And they – the grandchildren – don't have anything to depend on or look forward to. And that's a bad situation for people to be in, and to expect an enlightened choice from people in that kind of trouble may be asking too much.

HELENA: Especially when there is no enlightened offer.

WENDELL: If there was an enlightened alternative the scene would be different. But I don't think any presidential candidate has a clue about the existence of rural America, much less the problems that it has.

HELENA: This is so frightening because throughout the world, in places like China, India, and most of Africa, you're seeing farmers being pulled and pushed off the land. They're told that rural life and they themselves are backward and primitive, and if they want to be respected they've got to move into the city. And by the million they're pouring into the cities – whether in their own country or in another country – where they're trying to get a job, but the jobs are not available. And the results include angry reactions that in many cases translate into local ethnic friction, and then into an anger and hatred against the West, even into terrorism. So there is a breakdown of really genuine local economies connected to the land – it's destruction in the name of progress and efficiency. We are now at a point where more than half of the global population has been urbanized. But we do have an opportunity to say in a loud voice "let's push the pause button on this juggernaut that's pulling people away from real livelihoods, and then start a journey back to the land." Not everyone has to live on the land, but we need cities that have a relationship with the land around them and that have some breathing space within them so that we regain that contact with nature and with the real source of our livelihoods – with the real economy.

WENDELL: We need people on the land who are capable of acting as a sort of lobby – to defend it, but also to use it well. These terrible problems that you're talking about come about because a depreciation of the humanity of these people has been necessary to their exploitation, to their use as colonies. If you're going to steal from somebody, you need to convince yourself that they're inferior and then you have to convince them that they're inferior. I've heard too many farmers in meetings who start to speak by saying, "I'm just a farmer and I don't know much." They've been told that, and it's false, and it's a terrible tragedy and depreciation that they've convinced themselves is true.

HELENA: And now it's, what, one-and-a-half percent in the US that are still farming?

WENDELL: I don't think anybody knows for sure – it's less than 1%, but you know the Census Bureau ceased a number of years ago to count farmers, because they're not a demographically significant population. And very few people who are still farming are making their living entirely from farming. They're working in town, or their spouses are working in town – something else is being done to support what you'd have to think of as their love for farming. If they didn't love it, they wouldn't do it.

HELENA: I was recently invited to be part of a brainstorming session with a group of environmentalists, climate activists and thinkers to identify root causes and key solutions for the future. And it was shocking to me that over three days, out of a group of twenty, I was the only one who referred to food and farming. And then the third time I tried to bring it up, someone said "well, I don't want to farm", and the unspoken group conclusion was "...therefore farming is not important."

WENDELL: (Laugh). This is probably an intelligent person saying something utterly stupid. Well, I think the only thing that's required is: if you're interested in food, and it's a legitimate interest, you have to be willing to follow it out as it branches into our economic life. We don't need everybody on the farm, God forbid, but we do need support from the city, and the use of the land needs to be much better staffed than it is. To say so implies a very painful need for patience; it's going to take a long time to get this done. But we need to help it along.

HELENA: Here too is where I really believe in the 'resistance and renewal' message, because I believe that the resistance part would involve a people's movement demanding policy change. Just last night I gave a talk at Schumacher College, and someone pointed out that David Korten had written in one of his books a long list of what over 70% of Americans agreed on. I think we all care about our community, our family, our friends, our health – we want a healthy climate and a healthy world. But in the left/right political theater we have today, none of these things are being addressed properly.

WENDELL: I think you and I are seeing things from a kind of agrarianism. This has nothing to do with the left and the right. This simply says that the land – the given world – is of ultimate value, and that the caretaking of it is a matter of paramount importance. To argue from those two points puts you outside the current political dialogue. We just have to accept that. But there are more and more people who do understand that. The county governments and city governments are coming to understand that. I don't think, in America, state governments and the national government can understand it at all. But the county judge in my county would understand our conversation perfectly. The governor of the state would think we were speaking a foreign language.

HELENA: Isn't that so interesting? It's a pattern that is quite logical, because at the level of the local council the leaders are responding to the realities on the ground – what people need and what the land needs. But when you go up to that higher level they're off in their own utopian make-believe world of numbers and statistics. Nevertheless, as you say, there is a waking up – I see awareness trickling upwards, and it's very encouraging – particularly when we know how pressured people have been and how suppressed. Media, government, funding – it's not been there to support this agrarian movement and this new farmers' movement. But also, to see a lot of young people now wanting to farm – isn't that the most inspiring thing of all?

WENDELL: Yes, it's inspiring that they want to. It's much more inspiring when they try it and are able to keep at it for, say, five years. Because there's a great difference between 'wanting to' and doing it, and between doing it and surviving at it. So there are some young people from an urban background who have taken up farming, and some of them are doing admirably but with difficulty, and that needs to be said. But as it trickles up we just have to make sure that it trickles up from things that actually work. From real knowledge down here at the bottom.

HELENA: What we do in our organization is to encourage people to really understand this global techno-economic monoculture so that they can be much more strategic as they start these projects. For instance, in South Korea, my book *Ancient Futures* was a bestseller and it sold half a million copies, and I've been told that it led to quite a movement back to the land among young people, but it was only in later years that I've been able to work with them and really make sure they've understood that I was saying they need a community – and that means don't go off and just think it's only about producing something on the land. Or if you're trying to live off the land, try to expand the number of people who are doing it with you. But it's particularly this understanding that we need a community.

WENDELL: The great weapon that the industrial food system has used against farmers is surplus production – and farmers will inevitably overproduce. There's no way to stop it without some kind of organization, some kind of policy, at some level. There are two reasons for overproduction. One is hope; the other is despair. For whichever reason, farmers produce all they can. And this deprives them of what people here might call an 'asking price'. When they go to town with their produce, do they have a price that they can demand, an asking price? And the answer is that over the long history of agriculture farmers have very rarely had an asking price. They've simply carried their produce to the market and accepted whatever they were offered. And that's where the enlightenment of the agricultural population has to begin - with the question: "Have you ever had an asking price?" Well, a great example of the right response to that is the tobacco program as it was organized here in my part of the country. It's too bad that it was tobacco because it carries that stigma, but it would work for any product. And it was simply a program that said "we will give you this much", and it was a livable income based on the principle of parity. But "we will only protect this much; you can only bring this much to market" – so it combined price supports with production control, and that's what you have to do, otherwise the farmers will just produce themselves into bankruptcy. That is to say, they'll succeed themselves into failure. And it gets worse as the ability to produce increases; and it gets worse as they give up subsistence economies.

HELENA: Because 'subsistence' also carries some stigma, the term I prefer is the 'diversified local or regional economy'. And of course all of the infrastructure and technologies which could be useful for that much more diversified, healthy economy has been either destroyed or marginalized or never even invented. There's still such a scope, isn't there, for genuinely appropriate technologies?

WENDELL: Value-adding industries to the products of the land don't have to be as big as an airplane factory. We now have a very good small slaughter facility, here in our county, again. And this opens up lots of opportunities. My daughter is trying to set up a beef co-op here to market for the farmers – in their interests. And it would be then processed here. Otherwise it goes out of the community without adding much to the benefit of the community. If our trees leave this community, as raw logs or rough lumber, the community doesn't benefit much.

HELENA: Also, in industrial society the system has driven up the price of human labor and artificially lowered the price of energy and technology, and through that encouraged every single enterprise to use more energy and technology while throwing more people on the rubbish heap. And if that could be shifted we would have a completely different economy; we would have a completely different world.

WENDELL: A cheap food economy is a disaster. But we've got to be careful in saying that. Food is too cheap from the standpoint of the producers. Still from the standpoint of poor consumers it's too high. So it's a complex matter, and we oughtn't to oversimplify.

HELENA: No, but it's pretty clear that so-called 'cheap' food is actually very expensive because of all the chemicals and energy involved in the food chain. Large numbers of people are employed not to farm, but in a whole series of destructive activities like developing new artificial flavors, additives, preservatives, GMOs, and people driving trucks across the country and then putting stuff in huge container ships – or even worse in airplanes – supporting a system in which countries routinely import and export the same products. In the meanwhile, others involved in the food chain are the speculators, sitting in front of computers seeking the best price wherever it may be. So there's a large amount of waste involved, and then this long-distance, processed, rather toxic food is offered at a lower price thanks to a whole range of direct and hidden subsidies. Meanwhile, the local food movement is demonstrating what can happen when you shorten distances: you encourage a shift from monoculture to diversification on the land, you reduce the energy consumption, the packaging, the refrigeration and the waste, you provide healthier food at a reasonable price, and you have healthier, more prosperous farming communities.

WENDELL: I was born into a way of farming that used solar energy. And I haven't forgotten it. We had these solar converters called mules, and human beings, and that's the way we got the work done. (Laugh).

HELENA: Wendell, remind me again how old you are...

WENDELL: Well, sometimes, Helena, I think I'm only about 20. But I'm 83.

HELENA: Well, you sound like 20 and I know you're strong and healthy like 20.

WENDELL: I'm not as strong and durable as I used to be by a long way, I can tell you that. I'm perfectly natural.

HELENA: Perfectly natural. (Laugh).

145

REFERENCES

1. Reclaiming the Future

1. David Pierson, "U.S. farmers making hay with alfalfa exports to China," *LA Times*, June 8, 2014.
2. Elisabeth Rosenthal, "Environmental Cost of Shipping Groceries Around the World," *New York Times*, April 26, 2008.

2. Globalization: Creating a Lose-Lose World

1. Jeffrey D. Sachs, *The Price of Civilization: Economics and Ethics After the Fall* (Toronto: Random House Canada, 2011), 94.
2. New York Times Editorial Board, "Race to the Bottom," *New York Times*, December 5, 2012. Also see: Louise Story, "As Companies Seek Tax Deals, Governments Pay High Price," *New York Times*, December 1, 2012; Philip Mattera, "Subsidizing the Corporate One Percent: Subsidy Tracker 2.0 Reveals Big-Business Dominance of State and Local Development Incentives," Good Jobs First, February 2014.
3. Edward Humes, "Your iPhone's 500,000 mile journey to your pocket," *Wired* magazine, April 12, 2016.
4. Robert Samuelson, "The new globalization", *Washington Post*, October 16, 2013. Note that as of 2017, cross-border flows are 1/3 that of 2007 levels; for updated statistics, see Susan Lund, "The new dynamics of financial globalization", McKinsey Global Institute, August 2017.
5. "Livestock and Meat International Trade Data," US Department of Agriculture Economic Research Service (USDA ERS), September 2018 (accessed October 5, 2018); "Data by Commodity – Imports and Exports; Commodity: Potatoes," USDA ERS, December 18, 2018 (accessed December 22, 2018). For up-to-date data, see: FAOSTAT (United Nations Food and Agriculture Organization), and "US Agricultural Trade Data Update," USDA ERS, updated frequently. Also see: Rianne C. ten Veen, "Global Food Swap," Greening the North, January 2011; Caroline Lucas, "Stopping the Great Food Swap: Re-localizing Europe's Food Supply," The Greens/European Free Alliance/ European Parliament, March 2001; Helena Norberg-Hodge, Todd Merrifield, and Steven Gorelick, *Bringing the Food Economy Home* (London: Zed Books, 2002), 18.
6. Paul Greenberg, "Why Are We Importing Our Own Fish?" *New York Times*, June 20, 2014.
7. Samuelson, op. cit.
8. Michael McLeay et al., "Money creation in the modern economy," Bank of England Quarterly Bulletin, 2014 Q1. See also: David Graeber, "The truth is out: money is just an IOU, and banks are rolling in it," *The Guardian*, March 18, 2014; Josh Ryan-Collins et al., *Where Does Money Come From?*

A guide to the UK monetary and banking system, New Economics Foundation, 2012.

9. "General Government Debt," Organization for Economic Cooperation and Development (OECD) Data (accessed April 2, 2019). See also: "How much is too much?" *The Economist*, June 3, 2015.

10. Duncan Green, "The world's top 100 economies: 31 countries; 69 corporations," People, Spaces, Deliberation, World Bank, Sept 20, 2016. See also: "State of Power 2014," Transnational Institute, 2014.

11. "The Top 10," Fortune Global 500, 2018; "The World Factbook," US Central Intelligence Agency, 2017 (accessed December 17, 2018).

12. "Fossil Fuel Subsidies: Overview," Oil Change International, updated October 2017.

3. Counting the Costs

1. Robert E. Scott, "NAFTA's Legacy," Economic Policy Institute, Dec 17, 2013.

2. Timothy A. Wise, "Agricultural Dumping Under NAFTA: Estimating the Cost of US Agricultural Policy to Mexican Producers," Woodrow Wilson International Center for Scholars, 2010.

3. Mark Weisbrot, et al., "Did NAFTA Help Mexico? An Update After 23 Years," Center for Economic and Policy Research, March 2017.

4. "How to... Oppose a Supermarket Planning Application," Friends of the Earth UK, September 2005.

5. $258 billion in retail sales projected for 2018 divided by 613,000 employees in the third quarter of 2018 equals approximately 23 employees per $10 million in retail sales. Sources: Ingrid Lunden, "Amazon's share of the US e-commerce market is now 49%, or 5% of all retail spend," Tech Crunch, July 2018; Felix Richter, "Amazon's Workforce is More than Half a Million Strong," Statista, November 1, 2018; Stacy Mitchell, "The Truth about Amazon and Job Creation," Institute for Local Self-Reliance, July 29, 2013.

6. Olivia Laveccia and Stacy Mitchell, "Amazon's Stranglehold: How the Company's Tightening Grip Is Stifling Competition, Eroding Jobs, and Threatening Communities," Institute for Local Self-Reliance, November 2016

7. John Vidal, "eco soundings", *The Guardian* (London and Manchester), September 6, 2000, "Society" section, 8

8. Stacy Mitchell, "The Truth about Amazon and Job Creation," Institute for Local Self-Reliance, July 29, 2013.

9. "Global advertising spending from 2010 to 2018 (in billion US dollars)," Statista, 2018; Corey McNair, "Global Ad Spending: the eMarketer forecast for 2018", eMarketer, May 4, 2018.

10. "Where the Admen Are," *Newsweek*, March 14, 1994, 34.

11. "Depression" (Fact sheet No. 369), *World Health Organization*, March 22, 2018.

12. Tony Dokoupil, "Why Suicide Has Become an Epidemic – and What We Can Do to Help," *Newsweek*, May 23, 2013.

13. Eric Chivian and Aaron Bernstein, eds., *Sustaining life: How human health depends on biodiversity*, Center for Health and the Global Environment, Harvard Medical School (New York: Oxford University Press, 2008).

14. Global Footprint Network Open Data Platform – United States of America, ecological footprint (number of earths), 2014, http://data.footprintnetwork.org/ (accessed April 3, 2019).

15. WTO and UNEP, *Trade and Climate Change: A report by United Nations Environmental Programme and the World Trade Organization* (Geneva: WTO Publications, 2009), 53.

16. Kirk Semple, "Mexico Ready to Play the Corn Card in Trade Talks," *New York Times*, April 2, 2017.

17. Jon Ungoed-Thomas, "British Prawns Go To China To Be Shelled," *The Sunday Times*, May 20, 2007.

18. "Far Flung Foods: Europe's Distant Diets," European Science Foundation, Dec 11, 2007.

19. "Livestock and Meat International Trade Data," USDA ERS, updated March 28, 2019 (accessed April 3, 2019).

20. "Each Country's Share of CO2 Emissions," Union of Concerned Scientists, updated October 11, 2018; Navroz K. Dubash and Ankit Bhardwaj, "Guest post: India's emissions will double at most by 2030," Carbon Brief, August 22, 2018.

21. "An Economy for the 99%," Oxfam International, January 16, 2017.

22. "Inequality," OECD, www.oecd.org/social/inequality (accessed December 19, 2018). Also see: *Trade and Development Report 2012*, United Nations Conference on Trade and Development (UNCTAD), 2012; Ricardo Fuentes-Nieva and Nick Galasso, "Working for the Few," Oxfam International, January 20, 2014; Richard G. Wilkinson and Kate Pickett, *The Spirit Level: Why More Equal Societies Almost Always Do Better* (New York: Bloomsbury Press, 2009).

23. Lorraine Woellert and Sharon Chen, "Widening Gap: China's Income Inequality Surpasses US, Posing Risk for the Leadership of Xi Jinping," *Taipei Times*, May 6, 2014.

24. Franz Wild, "From Dainfern to Diepsloot: A short trip across SA's wealth gap," *Mail & Guardian*, May 7, 2014.

25. "Slum Almanac 2015/2016," UN Habitat, October 9, 2016.

26. Sasha Chavkin et al., "How the World Bank Broke Its Promise To Protect The Poor," The International Consortium of Investigative Journalists (ICIJ), April 16, 2015.

27. "The Urban Disadvantage: State of the World's Mothers 2015," Save the Children Federation, 2015.

28. Ian Johnson, "China's Great Uprooting: Moving 250 Million Into Cities," *New York Times*, June 15, 2013.

29. Mike Davis, "In New Economy, Textile Workers Hang by a Thread," *Los Angeles Times*, September 5, 2004.

30. From an FAO study based on 150 country reports. *State of the World's Plant Genetic Resources for Food and Agriculture*, FAO (Rome: FAO, 1996).

31. "Agropoly: a handful of corporations control world food production," Berne Declaration & Econexus, September 2013.

32. Frances Moore Lappé, "Farming for a Small Planet," Local Futures (blog), January 9, 2018.

4. The Rise of Extremism

1. Martin Hart-Landsberg, "Confronting Capitalist Globalization," Reports from the Economic Front (blog), December 16, 2016.

5. Localization – Getting from Here to There

1. "Towards an Alternative Trade Mandate for the EU," Alternative Trade Mandate, 2015. Page is archived; see the May 15, 2015 version of http://www.alternativetrademandate.org/resources/ (originally accessed September 23, 2015; accessed through Wayback Machine December 28, 2018).

2. "Rights for People, Rules for Corporations," StopISDS.org, https://stopISDS.org (accessed April 3, 2019).

3. Stacy Mitchell, "How State Banks Bring the Money Home," *Yes! Magazine*, September 23, 2011.

4. "Genuine Progress Indicator," Center for Sustainable Economy and the Institute for Policy Studies. Page is archived; see the July 20, 2014 version of http://genuineprogress.net/genuine-progress-indicator/ (originally accessed July 25, 2014; accessed through Wayback Machine December 29, 2018).

5. Ida Kubiszewski et al., "Beyond GDP: Measuring and achieving global genuine progress," *Ecological Economics* 93 (September 2013): 57-68; Claudio O. Delang and Yi Hang Yu, *Measuring Welfare beyond Economics: The Genuine Progress of Hong Kong and Singapore* (London: Routledge, 2015); Daniel Caixeta Andrade and Junior Ruiz Garcia, "Estimating the Genuine Progress Indicator (GPI) for Brazil from 1970 to 2010," *Ecological Economics* 118 (October 2015): 49-56; Marta Ceroni, "Beyond GDP: US states have adopted genuine progress indicators," *The Guardian*, September 23, 2014.

6. "No. 113. An act relating to the genuine progress indicator (S.237)," Vermont State Legislature, 2012, VT LEG 280576.1.

7. "Bhutan PM Casts Doubts Over Gross National Happiness," BBC News, August 2, 2013.

8. David Funkhouser, "How Much Do Renewables Actually Depend on Tax Breaks?" State of the Planet, Columbia University Earth Institute, March 16, 2018.

9. Rob Jordan, "Stanford researcher maps out alternative energy future for New York," Stanford Report, March 12, 2013.

10. Muhammad Musa, S. M. Bokhtiar, and Tayan Raj Gurung (Eds.), "Status and future prospect of organic agriculture for safe food security in SAARC countries," SAARC Agricultural Centre, December 2015.

11. "Bill to Promote Local Food Passes Final Vote," Ontario Ministry of Agriculture, Food and Rural Affairs, November 5, 2013.

12. Center for Good Food Purchasing, https://goodfoodpurchasing.org/ (accessed December 18, 2019).

13. Rodger Cooley, "Chicago Food Policy Action Council applauds Cook County adoption of Good Food Purchasing Program," Good Food Purchasing Program, May 16, 2018.

14. Eleanor Ainge Roy, "South Pacific islands ban western junk food and go organic," *The Guardian*, Feb 2, 2017.

15. "Cottage Food Laws," http://forrager.com/laws/ (accessed 18 December 2018).

16. Jula Bayly, "One Year After Becoming Law, Food Sovereignty in Maine has Taken Hold," *Bangor Daily News*, November 26, 2018; text from "The Maine Food Sovereignty Act," Maine Legislature, 2017, c. 314, §1.

17. Kimiko de Freytas-Tamura, "Welsh Town Leads a British Revolt Against the Tax System and Corporations," *The New York Times*, February 21, 2016; Rebecca Rutt, "The Welsh town that has moved its local businesses 'offshore' to shame HMRC into tackling tax-avoidance of Amazon and Google..." ThisisMoney.co.uk, January 20, 2016.

6. Grassroots Inspiration

1. Ken Tumin, "How Did The Financial Crisis Affect Credit Union Market Share?" DepositAccounts.com (accessed April 10, 2019).

2. Margrit Kennedy, Bernard Lietaer, and John Rogers, *People Money – the Promise of Regional Currencies* (Devon, UK: Triarchy Press, 2012), 27.

3. Slow Money, https://slowmoney.org/about (accessed December 28, 2018). See also: Michael Shuman, "24 Ways to Invest Locally," Post Carbon Institute, October 11, 2013; Michael Shuman, "Invest Locally: put your money where your life is," *Yes! Magazine*, June 5, 2009.

4. "About CTTE," Cape Town Talent Exchange (accessed April 4, 2019); "Trading without Money," http://learningclan.net/trading/ (accessed April 4, 2019); "Talent Market – Saturday March 30, 2019," Cape Town Talent Exchange (accessed April 4, 2019); "What is the CES?" Community Exchange System (accessed April 4, 2019).

5. Local Futures promoted local currencies starting in the 1990s, and sponsored two from our offices in Berkeley and Vermont. Our experience, and that of other local currency organizers over the years, is that these initiatives are generally best able to address only a narrow range of services – like babysitting and massage – and are generally not able to meet

other needs. Alternative currencies seem to work best when they are adjuncts to local food projects, and can also be successful in specific settings like ecovillages, festivals or ride-sharing programs.

6. Joseph Pisani, "McDonald's plans to nearly double restaurants in China," *USA Today*, August 8, 2017; Matt Rosenberg, "Number of McDonald's Restaurants Worldwide," ThoughtCo., February 11, 2018, with data from the McDonald's Corporation website.

7. "Sharing the sun: Community solar gardens taking off around the US," Energy Sage, January 3, 2018. "Evergreen Energy Solutions," Evergreen Cooperative Corporation, 2016 (accessed April 9, 2019); "Community Solar FAQ," Cooperative Energy Futures (accessed April 9, 2019).

9. Energiewende Team, "The Re-Municipalization of the Hamburg Grid," Energy Transition, June 27, 2014.

10. Naomi Klein, "Boulder, Colorado vs. Xcel Energy," https://solutions.thischangeseverything.org/ (accessed April 9, 2019). Adapted from *This changes everything: Capitalism vs. the climate* (Simon and Schuster, 2015).

11. Shay Castle, "Boulder moves forward with municipal utility as Xcel sets clean energy goals," Daily Camera *Boulder News*, December 5, 2018.

12. Laura Wisland, "Community Choice Aggregation Puts Communities in Control of Their Electricity", Union of Concerned Scientists, 10 Sept 2018.

13. "Our Work," Resilient Power Puerto Rico, https://resilientpowerpr.org (accessed April 10, 2019).

14. "Community Supported Agriculture," USDA National Agricultural Library, September 2018.

15. "National Count of Farmers Market Directory Listing Graph: 1994-2014," USDA Agricultural Marketing Service, 2014; "About Farmers Markets," Farmers Market Coalition, 2018, with data from USDA National Farmers Market Directory.

16. Alicia Miller, "Making Markets Mainstream," Sustainable Food Trust, June 23, 2014.

17. Helga Willer and Julia Lernoud, "World of Organic Agriculture Statistics and Emerging Trends 2018," FiBL & IFOAM – Organics International, February 2018.

18. "About the Farm" and "Fall Failures," Four Root Farm, http://www.fourrootfarm.com/ (accessed April 3, 2019).

19. American Farmland Trust, "Farms Under Threat: The State of America's Farmland," May 9, 2018.

20. Agrarian Trust, https://agrariantrust.org (accessed April 3, 2019).

21. "National Young Farmers Coalition 2017 Annual Report," National Young Farmers Coalition, 2017.

22. "The International Peasant's Voice," La Via Campesina, 2018 (accessed December 18, 2018).

23. "Declaration: La Via Campesina International Youth Coordination Meeting," La Via Campesina, May 13, 2011.

24. "Community Network Map," Institute for Local Self-Reliance, muninetworks.org, January 2018 (accessed December 18, 2018).

25. "What is Forest School?" Forest School Association (accessed April 3, 2019).

26. Shikshantar, http://www.shikshantar.org/ (accessed April 2, 2019).

27. Didi Pershouse, "Sustainable Medicine Manifesto", The Center for Sustainable Medicine, 2007.

28. Global Ecovillage Network, https://ecovillage.org/ (accessed December 18, 2018).

29. "About Repair Café," https://repaircafe.org/ (accessed April 3, 2019).

30. Community Environmental Legal Defense Fund, http://celdf.org/ (accessed December 18, 2018).

31. "About the Landworkers' Alliance," Landworkers' Alliance, 2017 (accessed April 3, 2019).

32. "Hidroeléctrica Puebla 1, Puebla, Mexico," Environmental Justice Atlas, February 1, 2017.

33. "Walmart Store in Cuetzalan, Puebla, Mexico," Environmental Justice Atlas, March 3, 2017.

34. Roberto Gonzalez Amádor, "Cuetzalan frenó a Wal-Mart; se impuso la economía real," *La Jornada*, April 25, 2012.

35. David Barstow, "Wal-Mart Hushed Up a Vast Mexican Bribery Case," *New York Times*, April 21, 2012.

36. María Luisa Albores, "Experiencia de Agroecología en la Tosepan...", *La Jornada del Campo*, December 17, 2016. See also: "Tosepantomin", Unión de Cooperativas Tosepan, 2016; "Yolseuiloyan: Donde el Corazón descansa y se fortalece", Unión de Cooperativas Tosepan, 2018.

7. Local Food for Our Future

1. "Who Will Feed Us? The Peasant Food Web vs. The Industrial Food Chain" 3rd edition, ETC Group, 2017.

2. Reynard Loki , "Corporate Food Brands Drive the Massive Dead Zone in the Gulf of Mexico," Truthout, August 28, 2018.

3. Natasha Gilbert, "One third of our greenhouse gas emissions come from agriculture," *Nature News*, October 31, 2012.

4. "Summary of Recall Cases in Calendar Year 2018," USDA Food Safety Inspection Service, January 14, 2019 (accessed April 11, 2019).

5. Maggie Koerth-Baker, "Big Farms are Getting Bigger and Most Small Farms Aren't Really Farms at All," FiveThirtyEight, November 17, 2016; "Factory Farms Destroy Communities," Socially Responsible Agriculture Project (SRAP), 2019 (accessed April 1, 2019).

6. Mike Davis, "Slum Ecology," *Orion Magazine* (accessed April 12, 2019). Adapted from *Planet of Slums* (London: Verso, 2006).

7. "Report of the Panel of Eminent Experts on Ethics in Food and Agriculture, Fourth Session 26-28 November 2007," FAO, 2007, https://tinyurl.com7y8ak9hj8

8. "FAO sounds alarm on loss of livestock breeds," FAO Newsroom, September 4, 2007, https://tinyurl.com/y8rufksr

9. Charles Siebert, "Food Ark," *National Geographic Magazine*, July 2011; "Protecting the Food Ark," Rural Advancement Foundation International-USA, July 7, 2011.

10. See for example Peter Rosset, "The Multiple Functions and Benefits of Small Farm Agriculture in the Context of Global Trade Negotiations, Policy Brief #4," Institute for Food and Development Policy, 1999; ETC Group, *op. cit.*

11. Pine Island Community Farm, http://www.pineislandfarmvt.com (accessed April 6, 2019).

12. "Régie agricole," Ville de Mouans-Sartoux, https://www.mouans-sartoux.net/la-regie-agricole (accessed April 6, 2019). See also: Sakoto Kishimoto, Olivier Petitjean, and Lavinia Steinfort, "Reclaiming Public Services: how cities and citizens are turning back privatisation," Transnational Institute, June 2017; Jofre Rodrigo et al., "Local authorities supporting access to land for farmers: stories from Europe," European Access to Land network, June 2017.

13. Jon Jandai, "Life is easy. Why do we make it so hard?" Filmed at TEDxDoiSuthep, Chiang Mai, Thailand, August 2011, video.

14. Pun Pun Center for Self-Reliance, http://www.punpunthailand.org/ (accessed March 20, 2017).

15. Jandai, *op. cit.*

16. Jandai, *op. cit.*

8. Countering the Objections

1. Damian Carrington, "Land taken over by foreign investors could feed 550m people, study finds," *The Guardian*, June 27, 2014.

2. Ian Johnson, "China's Great Uprooting: Moving 250 Million Into Cities," *New York Times*, June 15, 2013.

3. "New Census Data Show Differences Between Rural and Urban Populations," United States Census Bureau, December 8, 2016; "Farm Demographics – U.S. Farmers by Gender, Age, Race, Ethnicity, and More," United States Department of Agriculture, May 2014.

4. John W. Day and Charles Hall, "The Myth of the Sustainable City," *Scientific American*, August 21, 2016.

5. "Take 'mosaic' approach to agriculture, boost support for small farmers, UNCTAD report urges," UNCTAD, press release September 17, 2013.

6. "Hungry for land: small farmers feed the world with less than a quarter of all land," *GRAIN*, May 28, 2014.

9. Globalization Revisited

1. "Special Update on Investor-State Dispute Settlement: Facts and Figures," UNCTAD Investment Policy Hub, IIA Issues Note, Issue 3, November 2017.

2. The first five examples in this list are adapted from this report: "A Transatlantic Corporate Bill of Rights: Investor privileges in EU-US trade deal threaten public interest and democracy," The Seattle to Brussels Network, Corporate Europe Observatory, and The Transnational Institute, June 3, 2013. Used here in accordance with the Creative Commons Attribution-Non Commercial-Share Alike 3.0 Unported License. Gabriel Resources v. Romania, see: Adam Cerna Clark, "Whose Sovereignty? Gabriel Resources v. Romania," *Huffington Post*, August 5, 2016; "Gabriel Resources v. Romania," UNCTAD Investment Policy Hub (accessed April 9, 2019).

3. David Ricardo, *On The Principles of Political Economy and Taxation* (London: John Murray, 1817).

4. One need look no further than the ruined economy of Venezuela to see what can happen to countries that fully embrace comparative advantage. For decades now, Venezuela's economic strategy was to sell oil – the one product it has a 'comparative advantage' in – and with the proceeds buy everything else it needed. Now that the price of oil has dropped, the food shelves are empty, and the economy is collapsing.

5. Elisabeth Rosenthal, "Environmental Cost of Shipping Groceries Around the World," *New York Times*, April 26, 2008.

6. Kathleen Willcox, "Mongolia, Cheese, and the Future of Dairy in the Era of Climate Change," Civil Eats, January 3, 2019.

7. Tom Coburn, "Treasure Map: The Market Access Program's Bounty of Waste, Loot and Spoils Plundered from Taxpayers," June 2012; Tad DeHaven, "Export Subsidies: Market Access Program," Mercatus Center at George Mason University, March 8, 2018.

8. Arthur MacEwan, "The Ex-Im Bank: 'Crony Capitalism'?" *Dollars & Sense*, September 10, 2014.

9. "Frequently Asked Questions" and "Concentration 1995-2017," Environmental Working Group Farm Subsidy Database, http://farm.ewg.org/ (accessed December 18, 2018).

10. "Megadeals," Good Jobs First, June 2018 (accessed December 18, 2018).

11. "Wal-Mart Subsidy Watch: How Wal-Mart Has Used Public Money in Your State," Good Jobs First, 2007; "Amazon: Taxpayer Subsidies Help Build Its Monopoly," Good Jobs First, 2018 (accessed December 18, 2018); Robert McCartney, "Amazon HQ2 to benefit from more than $2.4 billion in incentives from Virginia, New York and Tennessee," *Washington Post*, November 13, 2018.

12. James Felkerson, "$29,000,000,000,000: A Detailed Look at the Fed's Bailout by Funding Facility and Recipient," Levy Economics Institute of Bard College, December 2011.

13. "Development banks back G20 global infrastructure hub," *Business Insider*, November 13, 2014.

14. Jeff Spross, "Global Ponzi Scheme: We're Taking $7.3 Trillion A Year In Natural Capital From Our Children Without Paying For It," Think Progress, April 23, 2013.

15. Damian Carrington, "Fossil fuels subsidised by $10m a minute, says IMF," *The Guardian*, May 18, 2015.

16. Richard Dobbs et al., "Infrastructure productivity: How to save $1 trillion a year," McKinsey Global Institute, January 2013.

17. Juliette Jowit, "World's top firms cause US$ 2.2tn of environmental damage, report estimates," *The Guardian*, February 18, 2010.

18. Robert Costanza et al., "Changes in the global value of ecosystem services," *Global Environmental Change* 26 (May 2014): 152–158.

19. Laura Beans, "New Study Traces Two-Thirds of Industrial Emissions to Just 90 Institutions," EcoWatch, November 21, 2013.

20. Gavin Stamp, "Counting the cost of the slave trade," *BBC News*, March 20, 2007; Balford Henry, "£7.5 trillion for slavery: Reparations commission says Ja would be due £2.3 trillion of total for caribbean," *Jamaica Observer*, September 22, 2014.

21. 'The WTO's financial services agreement will enter into force as scheduled," World Trade Organization, WTO NEWS, press release February 15, 1999.

22. David C. Korten, *Agenda for a New Economy*, (San Francisco: Berrett-Koehler), 21.

23. McLeay, *op. cit.* See also: Graeber, *op. cit.* and Ryan-Collins, *op. cit.*

24. "OTC derivatives statistics at end-June 2018," Bank for International Settlements, Oct 31, 2018. For additional discussion on the implications of high derivatives, see: "Why Derivatives May Be the Biggest Risk for the Global Economy," *Time* magazine online, March 27, 2013.

25. "Warren Buffet on Derivatives" (excerpts from the Berkshire Hathaway annual report for 2002), https://www.fintools.com/docs/Warren%20Buffet%20on%20Derivatives.pdf (accessed April 10, 2019). See also: Jeff Cox, "The value of what Buffett called 'financial weapons of mass destruction' is plunging," *CNBC News*, May 4, 2018.

26. "Debt and (not much) deleveraging," McKinsey Global Institute, February 2015.

27. Robert J. Samuelson, "The 247 Trillion Global Debt Bomb," *Washington Post*, July 15, 2018.

28. Felicity Lawrence, "Global food crisis: the speculators playing with our daily bread," *The Guardian*, June 2, 2011.

29. Ken-Hou Lin and Donald Tomaskovic-Devey, "How Financialization Leads to Income Inequality," Institute for New Economic Thinking, October 17, 2014.

30. US Debt Clock, http://www.usdebtclock.org (accessed December 14, 2018).

31. See, for example, Greece: 'Greece's Austerity Measures', BBC News, May 5, 2010; 'Financial Assistance to Greece', European Commission, updated November 2018 (accessed December 22, 2018).

32. Bill Moyers and Michael Winship, "Don't Let Net Neutrality Become Another Broken Promise," *Huffington Post*, July 5, 2014.

33. T.W. Farnam, "Study shows revolving door of employment between Congress, lobbying firms," *Washington Post*, September 13, 2011.

34. Citizens Trade Campaign, "What Corporations Want with the TPP," www.flushthetpp.org/tpp-corporate-insiders (accessed December 23, 2018).

35. C. Robert Gibson and Taylor Channing, "Here's how much corporations paid US Senators to fast-track the TPP bill," *The Guardian* (US edition), May 27, 2015.

10. Rethinking the Past

1. Columbus said of the Arawaks, "They were well-built, with good bodies and handsome features… so free with their possessions that no one who has not witnessed them would believe it. When you ask for something they have, they never say no." Howard Zinn, *A People's History of the United States* (HarperCollins, 2003). Also see: Marshall Sahlins, *Stone Age Economics* (Routledge, 1974). For a debunking of the supposed drudgery of pre-modern life in Europe, see Juliet Schor, *The Overworked American* (Basic Books, 1992).

2. "Over half of Sweden's households made up of one person," Eurostat (European Commission), September 5, 2017.

3. Loneliness has been described as a "public health crisis", and living alone is correlated with increased risk for alcohol-related death, depression, and suicide. See Jena McGregor, "This former surgeon general says there's a 'loneliness epidemic' and work is partly to blame," *Washington Post*, October 4, 2017. For correlation with alcohol-related death, see: "Living alone is associated with an increased risk of alcohol-related deaths," *EurekAlert!*, American Association for the Advancement of Sciences (AAAS), September 20, 2011. For correlation with depression, see: "People living alone are 'more depressed,'" *BBC News*, March 23, 2012. For correlation with suicide risk, see: Barbara Schneider et al., "Living alone, obesity, and smoking increase risk for suicide independently of depressive mood findings from the population-based MONICA/KORA Augsburg cohort study," *Journal of Affective Disorders* 152-154 (January 2014): 416-21

ABOUT THE AUTHOR

Author and filmmaker Helena Norberg-Hodge is a pioneer of the local economy movement. Through writing and public lectures on three continents, she has been promoting an economics of personal, social and ecological well-being for four decades. She is a widely respected analyst of the impact of the global economy and international development on local communities, local economies, and personal identity, and is a leading proponent of localization, or decentralization, as a means of countering those impacts. For this work she was awarded the prestigious Goi Peace prize in 2012 and the Arthur Morgan award in 2017.

Her inspirational classic, *Ancient Futures*, together with a film by the same title, has been translated into more than 40 languages, and sold over half a million copies. She is also the producer and co-director of the award-winning film, *The Economics of Happiness*. Helena has written numerous articles, essays, and book chapters, and is the co-author of two groundbreaking books on food and farming: *Bringing the Food Economy Home* and *From the Ground Up: Rethinking Industrial Agriculture*.

The *Earth Journal* counted Helena among the world's "ten most interesting environmentalists", while Carl McDaniel's book *Wisdom for a Liveable Planet* profiled her as one of "eight visionaries changing the world". Since 1975, she has worked with the people of Ladakh, or 'Little Tibet', to find ways of enabling their culture to meet the modern world without sacrificing social and ecological values. For these efforts she was awarded the Right Livelihood Award, or 'Alternative Nobel Prize'.

Educated in Sweden, Germany, Austria, England and the United States, Helena specialized in linguistics, including studies at the University of London and with Noam Chomsky at MIT. She has lectured in seven languages at numerous universities including Oxford, Harvard, Melbourne, Tokyo, Stockholm and Munich, and was Regents' Lecturer in the Energy and Resources Group at the University of California, Berkeley. She has also taught regularly at Schumacher College and appeared in broadcast, print and online media worldwide, including MSNBC, *The London Times*, *The Sydney Morning Herald* and *The Guardian*.

Helena is the founder/director of Local Futures and The International Alliance for Localization (IAL). She is also a founding member of the International Commission on the Future of Food and Agriculture, the International Forum on Globalization and the Global Ecovillage Network.

LOCAL FUTURES MATERIALS

FILMS:

The Economics of Happiness (2011)
Award-winning documentary describing the hidden costs of globalization and the multiple benefits of localization. Featuring interviews with Bill McKibben, Vandana Shiva, Richard Heinberg, Rob Hopkins, David Korten, Helena Norberg-Hodge and others, as well as inspiring stories of localization initiatives from around the world. 68 minutes.

Ancient Futures: Learning from Ladakh (1993)
Award-winning documentary based on the classic book. 60 minutes.

Paradise with Side Effects (2004)
Follows two Ladakhi women on a trip to England as part of a Local Futures 'reality tour.' Directed and produced by Claus Schenk, originally for German and French television. 40 minutes.

Local Futures: Beyond the Global Economy (1996)
Looks at Local Futures' systemic approach to the problems of the global economy, including hands-on work in Ladakh. 30 minutes.

The Future of Progress: Reflections on Environment & Development (1992)
A compilation of interviews with Edward Goldsmith, Martin Khor, Vandana Shiva, and Helena Norberg-Hodge. A concise and powerful challenge to prevailing theories of development. 30 minutes.

BOOKS & REPORTS:

Ancient Futures (Local Futures, 2016)
A moving portrait of tradition and change in Ladakh, or 'Little Tibet,' Ancient Futures is also a scathing critique of the global economy and a rallying call for economic localization. Originally published in 1991, this 2016 edition contains a new preface by the author, as well as the original foreword by H.H. the Dalai Lama, and an afterword by Peter Matthiessen. 210 pp.

Climate Change or System Change? (Local Futures, 2015)
An action report on the root causes of the climate crisis, and meaningful steps to address it. PDF, 16 pp. Free download at www.localfutures.org.

Localization: Essential Steps to an Economics of Happiness (Local Futures, 2015)
In-depth analysis of the global monoculture and the systemic benefits of a shift towards the local. Describes ways to resist further globalization

and to renew communities and local economies. PDF, 36 pp. Free download at www.localfutures.org.

Bringing the Food Economy Home: Local Alternatives to Global Agribusiness (Kumarian, 2002)

A concise description of the structures and costs of the global food system, and the many benefits of local food systems. 150 pp.

A Journey to New York (1996)

Local Futures' counter-development comic book. Follows a young Ladakhi boy who has become dismissive of his own culture and dreams of living in the West. He gets his wish, then finds out what life in the 'modern' world is really like. 32 pp.

Small is Beautiful, Big is Subsidized (ISEC, 1996)

A report on how government policies systematically support the large and global at the expense of the small and local. 56 pp.

From the Ground Up: Rethinking Industrial Agriculture (Zed Books, 1993)

A concise overview of the hidden costs of industrial food production, and prescriptions for a more ecological agriculture. 120 pp.

The Future of Progress: Reflections on Environment and Development (Resurgence, 1992)

A collection of 22 essays on the impacts of – and alternatives to – conventional development, the industrial model, and 'progress'. Contributors include Edward Goldsmith, Gary Snyder, Mohamed Idris, Vandana Shiva, Helena Norberg-Hodge and many others. 255 pp.

ABOUT LOCAL FUTURES

Local Futures (formerly the International Society for Ecology and Culture) works to renew ecological, social and spiritual well-being by promoting a systemic shift towards economic localization. An internationally respected advocate for new economies, Local Futures has been raising awareness about this issue for four decades.

Through its flagship Economics of Happiness program, Local Futures provides communities with a range of educational and practical tools for shifting direction – away from dependence on global monopolies, and towards decentralized, regional economies. The award-winning film *The Economics of Happiness* (2011) is the centerpiece of this program, and continues to be screened regularly throughout the world. Local Futures also organizes a series of conferences every year under the Economics of Happiness banner, providing an international forum for localization advocates from diverse parts of the world to connect with each other.

Local Futures began as The Ladakh Project in 1978, and initially focused on supporting Ladakh's indigenous culture by exposing the idealized images of Western consumer culture that were flooding into the region through tourism and development. Together with Ladakhi leaders, Local Futures established the first NGOs in the region, promoted organic agriculture, and developed a range of renewable energy technologies.

Since then, Local Futures has undertaken and supported numerous grassroots initiatives in both the global North and South. As a 'think-and-do tank', Local Futures produces books, films, online materials, study group curricula, and even comic books about strengthening ecological and social well-being, and organizes conferences, workshops, and public lectures to disseminate the global-to-local perspective. One of the first NGOs worldwide to promote local food, Local Futures is still almost unique in doing so from an international perspective. It has produced several books and numerous reports critiquing industrial food and promoting local alternatives, and its multi-media *Local Food Toolkit* won the Derek Cooper Award for Investigative Journalism.

Today, Local Futures operates from offices in the US, UK, Mexico and Australia, with 'sister' organizations in Germany and Japan.

LOCAL FUTURES
www.localfutures.org